Achievin...

Meeting the Professional Standards Framework

Teaching Primary

Special Educational Needs

Achieving QTS
Meeting the Professional Standards Framework

Teaching Primary

Special Educational Needs

Jonathan Glazzard, Alison Hughes,
Annette Netherwood, Lesley Neve
and Jane Stokoe

www.learningmatters.co.uk

Acknowledgements

Figure 3.1 reproduced by kind permission of Crown Copyright under Click-use Licence

First published in 2010 by Learning Matters Ltd

British Library Cataloguing in Publication Data
A CIP record for this book is available from the British Library.

ISBN 978 1 84445 367 2

This book is also available in the following ebook formats:
Adobe ebook ISBN: 9781844456833
EPUB ebook: ISBN: 9781844456826
Kindle ISBN: 9781844459827

Cover design by Toucan Design
Text design by Code 5 Design Associates
Project Management by Deer Park Productions, Tavistock
Typeset by PDQ Typesetting Ltd, Newcastle-under-Lyme
Printed and bound in Great Britain by Cromwell Press Group, Trowbridge, Wiltshire

Learning Matters Ltd
33 Southernhay East
Exeter EX1 1NX
Tel: 01392 215560
info@learningmatters.co.uk
www.learningmatters.co.uk

Contents

The authors

Jonathan Glazzard

Jonathan Glazzard has overall responsibility for Initial Teacher Training in Primary Education at the University of Huddersfield. He is course leader for the Primary QTS route and also teaches on the MA programme. Jonathan has worked at the University of Huddersfield since 2005. Prior to this, he worked as a primary school teacher and Assistant Headteacher in Barnsley for 10 years. During his time in schools Jonathan was responsible for the co-ordination of special educational needs. In addition to leading the Primary QTS course at Huddersfield, Jonathan teaches special and inclusive education at the university. He is currently using narrative approaches to research inclusive education for his doctoral thesis.

Alison Hughes

Alison Hughes became a Senior Lecturer at the University of Huddersfield on the BA (Hons) Early Primary Education following a successful teaching career lasting 34 years. She was a teaching head of a primary school for 11 years, during which time she worked with colleague heads on a number of collaborative partnerships and was a facilitator for the NCSL Leading Small Primary Schools programme. She has had a wide range of other teaching experiences which includes working with Reception, Key Stage 1 and Key Stage 2 children. She has a strong interest in special educational needs and spent some time as Teacher-in-Charge of a Hearing Impaired Unit. Earlier in her career she also worked in secondary education in Bradford, Inner London and Bedford.

Annette Netherwood

Annette Netherwood is a Lead Teacher in an all-age, all-inclusive special school in South Yorkshire, and a sessional lecturer at Huddersfield University, delivering lectures on special needs to QTS trainees. Annette has extensive experience of special needs in both mainstream and special schools. She obtained her MA in Action Research through exploring effective teaching and learning methods for SEN pupils. She has contributed to The Institute of Citizenship's work on the teaching of citizenship to SEN pupils. She has also been a research associate for the National College for School Leadership, leading to the publication of research, which explored innovative curriculum design. Annette works closely with a wide range of professionals and is fortunate in being able to expand her expertise and knowledge through their support and training.

Lesley Neve

Lesley Neve is a Senior Lecturer at the University of Huddersfield with long teaching experience across all phases of education. In more recent years she has specialised in working in teacher training both within the Foundation Stage and Key Stage 1 and also for the Lifelong Learning sectors. In addition to working with the trainees at Huddersfield, Lesley places the students on a special needs placement. Her interests include accessibility and integrating technology into mainstream settings. As a sufferer from dyslexia herself, Lesley has also previously worked as a SENCO.

Jane Stokoe

Jane Stokoe is a primary teacher with over 30 years' teaching experience across all phases of primary education. In more recent years she has specialised in working within the

Foundation Stage and Key Stage 1. Until recently she was leader of Foundation Stage and Key Stage 1 and is now enjoying the challenges of being an assistant head with the role of SENCO in a primary school in Barnsley. She works in partnership with the University of Huddersfield to support trainee teachers, a role that she greatly values. Additional experiences include working with and supporting a range of Early Years settings in the implementation of effective practice in the delivery of synthetic phonics. Jane has worked throughout her career to develop appropriate inclusive practices for all children and is committed to developing strategies to support the needs of learners with special educational needs.

Introduction

About this book

Every teacher needs to have detailed knowledge and understanding of special educational needs in order to provide inclusive education for the children they teach. The first key judgement, *Ofsted Framework for School Inspection* (2009): Pupils' achievement and the extent to which they enjoy their learning, makes specific reference to the quality of learning for pupils with special educational needs and/or disabilities and their progress. The Training and Development Agency for Schools has developed new teaching resources to increase trainees' understanding of special educational needs for initial teacher training. This book has been written to support the needs of all primary trainees on all courses of initial teacher training in England and other parts of the UK where a secure knowledge of Special Educational Needs is required for the award of Qualified Teacher Status (QTS) or its equivalent.

The features of this book include:

- clear links with the Professional Standards for QTS;
- knowledge and understanding of the most common reasons why a child may have a special educational need;
- case studies;
- practical tasks;
- reflective tasks;
- further reading.

Overview of chapters

Chapter 1: Inclusion: Policy agenda and legislation
This chapter gives a brief history of policymaking from the mid-twentieth century to the present day. It emphasises that inclusive education reflects a commitment to all children, which demands a radical transformation of the curriculum and assessment systems and that all teachers need to take seriously their responsibility for the education of all children.

Chapter 2: The Special Educational Needs Code of Practice
The Code of Practice is outlined and its implications for the education of children with special educational needs are discussed.

Chapter 3: Learning and cognition
This chapter explores what it meant by 'learning' and 'cognition'. It considers a range of theories about cognition that inform current thinking about how children learn. The nature of learning difficulties is discussed and specific difficulties defined. Finally, a range of teaching strategies are suggested to support teaching and learning.

Chapter 4: Supporting children with reading difficulties
This chapter focuses on dyslexia and provides examples of strategies for supporting

children who fall within this group. Many children with general reading difficulties will have similar problems to those who are dyslexic. The distinction between those who are dyslexic and those with reading difficulties will be explored further in this chapter. Social models of disability are discussed. The impact of dyslexia on children's self-esteem is examined, as are strategies for developing a dyslexia-friendly learning environment.

Chapter 5: Speech and language
Some of the main issues around the acquisition of speech and language, its importance as a means of communication and as a tool for thinking are explored in this chapter. It describes how language is constructed in our society and how this may be different to how it is constructed in other communities which may impact on children with English as an additional language (EAL). Effective communication in the classroom is explored and suggestions made as to how this may be used to differentiate the language learning for children with speech, language and communication needs (SLCN) including the use of effective questioning. It examines how a range of SLCN difficulties can impact on language development and suggests some strategies to aid the language learning of these children.

Chapter 6: Supporting children with autistic spectrum disorders
Children with autism are often discussed as though they represent a homogenous group of learners. Strategies to support the learning and development of these children will need to be as diverse as the needs of each learner. Warnock (2005) has highlighted key issues associated with the inclusion of autistic children into mainstream learning environments. These concerns will be discussed in this chapter. It goes on to provide an overview of the evolution of the concept of autism and highlights the challenges faced by this diverse group. Practical strategies for supporting children with autism are discussed.

Chapter 7: Supporting children with behavioural, emotional and social difficulties
Children do not come to school as 'empty vessels'. Irrespective of their background all children are shaped by their social environment, and while for most this has a positive impact on their learning within school, for some it can sadly be a barrier. It is often argued that social, emotional and behavioural problems have their roots in 'nurture' rather than 'nature'. This chapter outlines how teachers, irrespective of the cause, have to support these pupils while maximising their educational potential.

Chapter 8: Developing partnerships with pupils and parents
This chapter considers the importance of providing pupils, parents, carers, practitioners and teachers with an equal voice. All parties have valuable contributions to make and by working together they will create strong building blocks for effective partnership.

Chapter 9: Developing partnerships with outside agencies
This chapter provides an overview of some of the outside agencies and the role they play in supporting the needs of the child. It discusses the need for multidisciplinary teams and how some of the issues surrounding how this might be put into practice.

Chapter 10: Creating learner-friendly environments
This chapter examines the importance of teachers reflecting on their own values in relation to special educational needs. In addition it considers ways in which teachers can modify learning objectives, vary teaching styles or use access strategies to enable learners with special educational needs to participate and achieve.

PART 1
UNDERSTANDING SPECIAL
EDUCATIONAL NEEDS

1
Inclusion: policy agenda and legislation

Chapter objectives

This chapter will enable you to:

- understand the development of inclusive education over the last 30 years;
- understand the meaning of inclusion and how inclusion differs from integration;
- know the key legislation and policy agendas which relate to inclusion;
- understand some of the theoretical frameworks which underpin disability.

This chapter addresses the following Professional Standard for the award of QTS:
Q3(a)

Introduction

This chapter introduces you briefly to the historical development of inclusive education. It examines definitions of inclusion and it considers the key barriers to the development of effective inclusive practice. The chapter addresses the medical and social models of disability and it draws on case studies from practice.

A potted history of the development of inclusive education

The 1972 Education Act gave all children the right to an education, however severe their disabilities. Following this Act many local education authorities struggled, without guidance, to provide school education for children with special educational needs and most of the education took place in special schools (Warnock, 2005). In 1974 Margaret Thatcher, then the Secretary of State for Education, commissioned the Committee of Inquiry into the Education of Handicapped Children and Young People to review the education of pupils with special educational needs. Mary Warnock led the inquiry and the recommendations from this were published in the Warnock Report in 1978. The report made the recommendation that, where possible, children with special educational needs should be educated in mainstream schools. The notion of 'integration' was born.

The recommendations of the Warnock Report formed the basis of the 1981 Education Act, which introduced a financial safety net to support the most vulnerable children in mainstream provision. This was to be known as the statement of special educational needs. However, the 1981 Education Act made no provision for any additional funding to be allocated to local education authorities for the new procedures (Warnock, 2005). Funding for the assessment of pupils with special educational needs and the issuing of statements was therefore nonexistent. The effect of this was that parents fought with cash-strapped local education authorities to gain statements for their children (Warnock, 2005). Tribunals were established in the 1990s to adjudicate in the disputes. Warnock has since stated that she personally feels that she holds *a degree of responsibility for what turned out to be not a very bright idea* (Warnock, 2005, 27) when referring to the statementing process. However, this self-criticism is perhaps too harsh given the fact that the purpose of the statement was to keep as many pupils as possible in mainstream schools as a result of meeting their needs.

The late 1980s and the 1990s witnessed the growth of the competitive market in which schools had to operate. The Education Reform Act of 1988 gave birth to the National Curriculum and this was accompanied with the introduction of statutory assessment tests (SATs) in primary and secondary schools. Results were displayed in league tables and these became a measure of school success. A system of rigorous school inspections was established during the 1990s and failing schools were named and shamed. Underperforming schools were placed in 'Special Measures' and subjected to a process of re-inspection and threat of closure unless results improved. This marketisation of schooling has not been conducive to the development of inclusive practices in schools, since schools with high numbers of pupils with special educational needs risk lower academic standards (Warnock, 2005). Thus, according to Warnock (2005, 21), *competition was to govern educational provision*.

Despite the climate of competition the Labour government continued the raising standards agenda when they came to power in 1997. However, they also advanced an agenda for inclusive education. The Green Paper (DfEE, 1997) and the subsequent Programme of Action (DfEE, 1998) recommended strategies aimed at supporting inclusion through early intervention, staff training, research to disseminate best practice, changes in the nature of local authority support and a revision of the Code of Practice (Cole, 2005). The Special Educational Needs and Disability Act (SENDA) in 2001 stated that schools had a statutory responsibility to plan for the inclusion of all children. This act made *the underlying assumption... that all children will ultimately attend mainstream schools* (Cole, 2005, 334). In the same year, the Disability Discrimination Act required schools to make *reasonable adjustments* (Cole, 2005, 334) to ensure that disabled pupils were not disadvantaged. The *Every Child Matters* (ECM) agenda emphasises inclusion and the right of all children to enjoy their education and to achieve. It encapsulates the government strategy for SEN, *Removing barriers to achievement* (DfES, 2004), which emphasises the need for early intervention, removing barriers to learning, raising expectations and achievement and delivering improvements in partnerships with other agencies. Effective multi-agency working is a key principle of the ECM agenda.

However, according to Goodley:

> *Educational environments, curricula content, teacher identities are all normatively associated with environments, standards and achievements that are at odds with the quirkiness of disabled learners. Schools continue to exclude children by virtue*

of their inaccessibility. Curricula promote standards that some with (or without) impairments will never reach...Teachers are assessed in ways that celebrate high achievement over the valuing of difference...disabled students continue to be singled out for specialized attention, are segregated from non-disabled peers through the presence of non-disabled adult supporters and remain unrepresented in images of schooling and educational attainment.

(Goodley, 2007, 319)

Therefore for children with special educational needs it is important to reflect on the extent to which current curricula and approaches to assessment marginalise and therefore exclude children with disabilities.

REFLECTIVE TASK

Discuss the following questions with a colleague on your course.

Is the current emphasis on literacy, numeracy and norms (standards) instrumentally failing certain groups of learners and allowing other learners to excel?

How could the current assessment system be modified to include different ideas of what constitutes success and achievement in order to become fully inclusive?

It's all in a name: arriving at a definition of inclusion

Booth *et al.* argue that:

...Inclusion is not another name for special educational needs...inclusion is seen to involve the identification and minimising of barriers to learning and participation and the maximising of resources to support learning and participation.

(Booth *et al.*, 2000, 13)

The role of participation in learning is clearly very important. Learning will be minimised if pupils fail to participate in the process of learning. However, this definition is limited in the sense that it does not emphasise the importance of pupils' achievement. Participation on its own is not enough. It is crucial that we have high expectations of all our pupils and provide them with learning opportunities, which help to maximise both their participation and achievement. Booth *et al.* are right to emphasise the fact that inclusion is about a deep concern for the education of all pupils, not just pupils with special educational needs. However, it is critical to stress that the main purpose behind minimising the barriers to pupils' learning is to maximise pupils' levels of achievement.

Other definitions of inclusive education have focused on viewing differences between pupils in a very positive way. According to Corbett and Slee:

Inclusive education is an unabashed announcement, a public and political declaration and celebration of difference. It requires continual proactive responsiveness to foster an inclusive education culture.

(Corbett and Slee, 2000, 134)

Schools which embrace the agenda for inclusion need to make fundamental changes to their policies, practices and culture in order to ensure that all pupils feel safe, valued and have a sense of belonging, allowing them to participate and achieve.

Some writers have been keen to emphasise that inclusive education is not just about the needs of pupils with learning disabilities or those classed as having special educational needs. Instead they stress that inclusive education stems from a deep concern for all pupils and their right to attend, participate and achieve in their local mainstream school (Slee and Allan, 2001). According to Carrington and Elkins (2005, 86), *above all, inclusion is about a philosophy of acceptance where all pupils are valued and treated with respect*.

However, other definitions stress that inclusion is not about all children attending a mainstream school. The government's perspective is that inclusion is not just about the school which a child attends but *the quality of their experience; how they are helped to learn, achieve and participate fully in the life of the school* (DfES, 2004, 25). In this respect, inclusion is not just viewed in locational terms but in social and curricular respects. Warnock (2005, 37) argues that *for some children participation is impossible in the context of the mainstream school*. She expresses that:

> *Inclusion is not a matter of where you are geographically, but of where you feel you belong. There are many children, and especially adolescents, identified as having special educational needs, who can never feel that they belong in a large mainstream school.*

> (Warnock, 2005, 38)

She also argues that some children with emotional, behavioural or cognitive difficulties:

> *...are genuinely unable to learn in a regular classroom, and...distract other children from learning if they are placed there. For these, the concept of inclusion is often stretched so that they are deemed to be included even if they attend classes in a special unit on the campus of the main school. But life on the school bus or in the school grounds may still be traumatic for them.*

> (Warnock, 2005, 39)

A rationale for inclusion

According to Florian (1998, 107), *the inclusion of all pupils in mainstream schools is part of an international human rights agenda which calls for the full inclusion of all people with disabilities in all aspects of life*. However, literature reviews on the benefits of inclusive education have tended to argue that the available evidence is inconclusive (Hornby, Atkinson and Howard, 1997; Farrell, 1997, Hunt and Goetz, 1997, Manset and Semmel, 1997; Feiler and Gibson, 1999; Hegarty, 1993).

Farrell (2001, 7) argues that *arguments in favour of inclusion based solely on human rights, powerful though they may sound, are logically and conceptually naïve*. Farrell defends the rights of parents to choose the right school for their child and the rights of mainstream pupils to receive a good education. Therefore the notion of rights is problematic and we must remember policy agendas should not supersede the rights of disabled pupils to express their own views about where they might wish to be educated.

PRACTICAL TASK PRACTICAL TASK **PRACTICAL TASK** PRACTICAL TASK **PRACTICAL TASK**

- Research the United Nations Convention on the Rights of the Child.
- Consider how you might incorporate this into your teaching.

Barriers to inclusion

Marketisation of schooling

Cole (2005, 332) is right to argue that *policies supporting inclusion are only one aspect of the educational policy landscape*. In addition to advancing an agenda for inclusion, New Labour has also advanced an agenda for raising standards. Barton (1998) refers to the creation of a quasi-market in education and it has been argued that this has produced a *potentially hostile context* (Fulcher, 1999, 151) for advancing an agenda for inclusion. Similarly, Slee (2001, 172) has argued that *the context of educational policy creates the conditions that militate against an inclusive educational project*.

The Education Act of 1986 and the Education Reform Act of 1988 both emphasised the role of parents as 'consumers' of education. The publication of school results in the form of league tables in the 1990s helped to fuel the competitive climate in which schools were operating. Corbett (1999) argues that the dominant ideology within the school effectiveness movement appears to suggest that effective schools are those which attain high examination results and appear near the top of the league tables. The appointment of School Improvement Officers in local education authorities, who are charged with raising school performance levels, supports this ideology. In addition to these pressures, government inspections of schools by the Office for Standards in Education (Ofsted) measure the success of a school by its results. Corbett (1999) argues that Ofsted's influence has not helped to foster an inclusive ideology in schools.

Thus, the increasing accountability of schools and the increasing emphasis on school performance have done little to encourage schools to embrace the inclusive education agenda. Corbett (1999, 59) has rightly argued that the league tables have set schools in competition with each other despite the fact that they *do not differentiate between schools with very few pupils who have learning disabilities and those with substantial numbers requiring additional support*. She argues that this has not encouraged schools to promote their commitment to less able learners. Corbett's argument has validity in the face of evidence that shows that schools are often keen to exclude children who, as a result of behavioural difficulties, are likely to underachieve (Howe and Welner, 2005). There is also evidence to suggest that some schools are reluctant to admit children who will fail to produce the desired results (MacLeod, 2001) and other research has found that some headteachers remain concerned about the impact of inclusion on their school's position in the league tables (Farrell, 2001). In addition to this, it has also been argued that schools may direct teaching input to those children who they define as 'borderline' cases (Feiler and Gibson, 1999). These are children who, with targeted support, will achieve the desired results. The effect of this is to direct attention away from the lower-achieving pupils, denying them the chance to achieve their potential. It has been argued that the inclusion agenda has to be located within broader education policies of raising standards and school improvement (Cole, 2005). However, some writers argue that the relationship between these policies is incompatible (Warnock, 1996; Barton, 1998; Armstrong, 1998). Cole (2005) has argued that this relationship will create winners and losers and some writers have claimed that the losers will be those children who are deemed as having special educational needs (Slee, 1996; Warnock, 1996; Barton, 1998).

There is also research which suggests that this quasi-education market has created tensions for many pupils, their teachers and parents, especially those who are concerned with the education of pupils with special educational needs (Gewirtz *et al.*, 1995; Barton, 1998). Slee and Allan (2005, 16) refer to the *marketisation of schooling*. Such a phrase encapsulates the fact that schools are now viewed as businesses where performance and outcomes are all-important and are indicators of success. In the current climate, pupils with learning disabilities are often pressurised into achieving academic targets, which will in turn improve school results. However, these targets may be inappropriate for these children, who are often forced to work under a model of education where it is deemed that 'one size will fit all'. Thus, although there may be locational inclusion in operation, social and curricular inclusion may be absent. This swims against the tide of inclusion.

The Audit Commission (2002) describes the dilemmas which schools face: *Schools feel pulled in opposite directions by pressures to achieve better academic results...and to become inclusive* (cited in Wedell, 2005, 4). Indeed, some would argue that the quest for inclusion and the political drive on academic standards are simply incompatible (Howe and Welner, 2005). They argue that *schools that include students who do not score well on the tests will be judged as inferior and, in the extreme, will be forced by the marketplace to close* (Howe and Welner, 37).

Vidovitch and Slee (2001) have rightly argued that educational policies of inclusion operate within a regime of accountability, which is inefficient, ineffective and socially unjust. Therefore if the government intends inclusion to succeed, it needs to review the criteria through which schools are judged. Examination results will always play a part in determining school effectiveness, but this should not be the only measure of a school's success.

Armstrong (2005), taking a sceptical view, argues that inclusion as a political agenda is a normative concept and is based on a policy aimed at establishing narrow cultural parameters of normality rather than being based on supporting the richness of social diversity. Thus, it could be argued that children with special educational needs are included in mainstream schools in order to normalise them. This argument contains seeds of logic. There is certainly evidence that some pupils who are included are made to follow inappropriate curricula and measured by the same performance indicators as the rest of the pupils. Inclusion for social justice, on the other hand, demands that schools restructure their policies and practices in order to provide all children with an education which is relevant to their needs.

Ineffective deployment of support staff

There is evidence to suggest that some students with special educational needs face isolation when they are included in mainstream educational environments (Ainscow *et al.*, 1999; Feiler and Gibson, 1999). These pupils are often supported by teaching assistants, which can result in:

...A new form of segregation within the mainstream, with the rather worrying dimension that some of the most challenging pupils are taught by the least qualified members of staff.

(Ainscow *et al.*, 1999, 138)

This is particularly worrying but not uncommon (Ainscow *et al.*, 1999). In addition, pupils with special educational needs are often singled out by being withdrawn from classrooms and taught on an individual level, thus inhibiting opportunities for peer interaction (Lewis, 1995). Wedell (2005) supports this view by arguing that:

The employment of learning support assistants (LSAs) for pupils with special educational needs has long been a means of 'softening the blow' for those who are in mainstream classes, but it is recognised that the 'velcro-ing' of LSAs to pupils sometimes actually becomes a form of within-class segregation.

(Wedell, 2005, 5)

REFLECTIVE TASK

Bearing in mind these viewpoints, how is the education of children with special educational needs managed in your own placement school or setting?

CASE STUDY

Inclusion: whose responsibility?

Peter was a child with global learning delay and dyspraxia. He had poor language and limited comprehension. Peter was taught within a mainstream classroom. Neither his class teacher nor his support assistant had received any training in his needs. The class teacher included Peter in social aspects of the class whenever possible and the other children responded well to this. Peter enjoyed being with his peers and often co-operated in these conditions. Peter was physically being educated in the same space as his peers. However, Peter was not able to access the work of his peers, a mixed Year 5/6 class, as he was operating on P scales. The class teacher prepared work for Peter, but this was the first year of Key Stage 2 SATs. Consequently it was frequently left to the classroom assistant to devise ways in which to educate Peter.

REFLECTIVE TASK

- Was Peter's education inclusive?
- How could the school have improved the teaching and learning for Peter?

Clearly, these practices are at odds with the ethos of inclusive education. There is also evidence of classroom teachers abdicating their responsibility for the education of pupils with special educational needs to other members of staff in the school (Farrell, 1998). Indeed, Rose is correct to assert that:

> *...Before inclusion can be achieved, it will be necessary for all teachers to accept a responsibility for the education of* all *pupils and to move away from depending upon support systems commonly found at present in schools.*
>
> (Rose, 2001, 148)

Dyson (1997) offers an interesting perspective that special education has merely *reproduced itself in a mainstream setting. It has, in other words, colonised rather than transformed the mainstream* (cited in Knight, 1999). Farrell, Balshaw and Polat (1999) have found that if classroom support assistants are well trained and supported in their duties, they offer the potential to make inclusion effective for a range of children with special educational needs.

PRACTICAL TASK PRACTICAL TASK **PRACTICAL TASK** PRACTICAL TASK **PRACTICAL TASK**

Think about a child who was successfully included in one of your placement schools. Identify:

- the child's difficulties and barriers to learning;
- strategies applied by the school to remove these barriers;
- key learning points for you from this experience.

Present this to your peers in the form of a five-minute presentation.

Staff training

According to Poulou and Norwich (2000, 305), *teacher professional development is a key factor in successful inclusion*. One of the most frequently cited barriers to inclusion is the lack of training that mainstream teachers receive in order to teach pupils with special educational needs (Minke *et al.*, 1996; Audit Commission, 2002). Included pupils are more likely to thrive when their teachers have the knowledge and ability to differentiate the curriculum in order to meet their individual needs (Ring and Reetz, 2000). Research has also found that inclusion is often inadequately addressed and often neglected in initial teacher training programmes (Barton, 2003; Booth *et al.*, 2003; Garner, 2001; Jones, 2002; Thomas and Loxley, 2001). According to Winter (2006, 89) *the consequence of this is that a large number of teachers may lack the confidence needed to meet the pupils' special needs*.

REFLECTIVE TASK

- Bearing in mind the viewpoints on teacher training in the above paragraph, how well do you feel your own ITT course prepares you to teach children with special educational needs?
- How might you work more closely with the Special Educational Needs Co-ordinator or Inclusion Co-ordinator to further your knowledge of children with SEN in the class you are placed in?

Labels

There is evidence that the use of labels to diagnose specific special needs can be extremely helpful for teachers, parents and pupils. Research by Riddick (1995) found that pupils with 'dyslexia' found the term useful as a way of explaining their difficulties, thus impacting positively on their self-esteem. The label provided the pupils with reasons for their difficulties and they no longer felt 'stupid' (Riddick, 1995). Within your practice you need to be careful not to let labels cloud your thinking. Not all children with autism need a visual timetable and not all children with dyslexia will respond positively to specific interventions. The danger of labels is that they encourage practitioners to perceive children who belong to a particular group as homogenous. Teachers need to remember that individual children will need individual strategies to support them.

Teacher expectations

Slee (2001) reminds us that inclusion starts with ourselves. Everyone involved in inclusion, therefore, needs to consider how far their own actions create barriers to inclusion (Allan, 2003). This is particularly important when evaluating our expectations of particular children. In their research, Rose and Shelvin (2004) interviewed children who were excluded from mainstream education. Low teacher expectations were a common theme to emerge out of the interview data. The researchers found that many of these pupils experienced success after leaving school, largely as a result of their own determination. Inclusion will not work unless teachers have high expectations of all pupils.

REFLECTIVE TASK

Think about the teachers you have worked with in your placement school(s).

- Did they display positive attitudes towards children with SEN and did they have high expectations of all children?
- How did their attitudes shape their practice in terms of how they worked with children with SEN, parents and outside agencies?

REFLECTIVE TASK

Think about how you included children with special needs while on a recent placement.

- Did you have high expectations of these children?
- How did you communicate these to the children?
- Were your learners successful?

Models of disability

According to Tregaskis (2002, 457), *the social model of disability has been an emancipatory force in the lives of many disabled people*. In this model, disability is seen as the result of economic, social and cultural oppression rather than the impairment itself being viewed as disabling. The assumption within the social model is that disability is a social construct. It makes a subtle but important distinction between disability and impairment, where disability is defined as a social construct and impairment is located within the body. It challenges the assumption that impairment will automatically lead to disability.

Defenders of the social model theory have argued that it has allowed disabled people to make sense of their own internalised oppression by enabling them to realise that they are not responsible for their own disablement (Tregaskis, 2002). The model shifts the blame for exclusion from the individual to society as a whole and places disabled peoples' functional capacities within a broader social and environmental context. It repositions people with impairments as citizens with rights and recognises the array of disabling barriers within society.

REFLECTIVE TASK

- Think carefully about how you might apply the social model of disability within your own practice. Can you think of any practical applications of this model?
- Can you think of examples from your placement schools where the social model of disability has been applied in practice?

CASE STUDY

Attitudes to inclusion

John was ten years old when he attended an autistic resource base, which was attached to a mainstream school. He had previously been excluded from several mainstream primary schools for presenting challenging behaviour and terrorising other pupils and staff. Even though John had no official diagnosis of autistic spectrum disorder, his previous school indicated that this was a possibility.

John's parents had found his behaviour at home very difficult to deal with. He regularly bullied his younger brother and he often attacked his parents. He frequently used abusive language and often refused to comply with parental expectations. Over a period of several years this had placed pressure on the family, particularly on his mother. He would display manipulative behaviour and would go to great lengths to 'get his own way'.

John had not responded well to his early mainstream education. He had been permanently excluded from two schools on account of his behaviour and the local authority appeared to be running out of options. A decision was made that resulted in John attending the autistic resource base at a local school, despite the fact that there had been no official diagnosis of autism. A review meeting confirmed that he would be partially included in the mainstream school on a 'trial' basis.

Very soon after John started in the resource base he began to terrorise the other children and attack the staff. Within weeks of him starting, he was given several fixed-term exclusions for his behaviour. After a month of him being at the resource base, a medical diagnosis confirmed that John was not autistic but in fact had a pathological personality disorder known as 'pathological demand avoidance'. This is a rare condition. As a result of this diagnosis, John was moved out of the resource base.

The medical professionals explained that the disorder had caused John to develop a sense of paranoia. He distrusted everyone. This paranoia resulted in him placing a padlock on his school lunch box so that no one could steal his food. John also developed several obsessions. One such obsession was that John did not want people to say specific words on particular days of the week. He stated what the 'forbidden' words were and if they were used, he would scream and tantrum, was very manipulative and was extremely good at instigating arguments that he was determined to 'win'.

The local authority had no suitable placement for John and no other local school wanted to admit him. The headteacher of the school eventually agreed to admit John on a temporary full-time basis, conditional on the local authority promising to fund two part-time teachers and two part-time support assistants. In addition to this the head asked the local authority to fund cover for a lunchtime supervisor who would oversee John during this part of the day. The staff who were employed to educate and supervise John were not experienced in working with children who had this condition.

Another barrier to effective inclusion was also established before the placement started. In view of John's behaviour, Sally, the class teacher, refused outright to teach John. She was concerned that his behaviour would present too many challenges and she argued that she had not had the necessary training to deal with it. She also expressed concern that John would impede the progress of the rest of the pupils. This was a particular worry for her, given the fact that the class were due to take their statutory tests at the end of the year.

John was not given a chance to prove himself. The head supported Sally and an agreement was made that John would be taught in his own room. His part-time teachers and his support staff would support him in a room next to Sally's.

John started his placement in the school. The classroom that he was placed in was not set up as a classroom. Initially John used the whole room. However, over a period of weeks he gradually withdrew into the carpet area of the classroom and this became 'John's den'. He barricaded the carpet area off with cupboards and screens and he insisted that all his lessons were to take place in this part of the room. He placed a table within his den and a set of drawers and this is where he 'worked' for the majority of the day. John would not allow other staff into his den. The only people who were privileged enough to be allowed access were the people who were responsible for supervising him. Initially, he did eat his lunch with the other children but very quickly he retreated into eating it within his den.

It became apparent that no structures were put into place for John. His teachers did not plan lessons for him. He was allowed to decide which activities to engage in and sometimes it was clear that he was not taking part in any educational activity at all. Initially he had visited the classrooms with the youngest children in and he enjoyed 'helping' them. However, after he had established his den, he no longer wanted to do this and he stopped visiting. He had also initially taken part in playtimes with other children. However, his constant swearing had resulted in them complaining and a decision was taken that John would have his own playtimes, supervised by his teachers and support staff.

One of John's teachers frequently had rows with him. She seemed to be confrontational and this made him worse. His lunchtime supervisor took on the role of 'doting' grandma, which John exploited by manipulating her. One day John had returned into his 'den' from an individual playtime to find that some art work had been left in his space. He responded by ripping up all the work. He suffered consequences for this and was publicly humiliated by the head, the deputy and one of his support teachers in front of the whole school. John's response to this was to retaliate and shout back at the head. In John's eyes his space had been violated and not respected.

After a review meeting to discuss transfer to secondary provision, it was decided that John would attend a local special school for pupils with severe behaviour problems. At his transition meeting the head of the school recommended that John would be best educated in his own classroom, with his own teachers. He was described as a severely disruptive child who needed to be kept apart from the other children for their own safety. The special school accepted this advice and set up a classroom where John would be educated on his own. John is still at the school and awaiting transfer to the special school.

REFLECTIVE TASK

- Reflect on the story you have just read. What were the barriers to John's inclusion?
- How was John's voice marginalised?
- How might the situation have been handled differently?

RESEARCH SUMMARY RESEARCH SUMMARY **RESEARCH SUMMARY** RESEARCH SUMMARY

Corbett and Slee's emphasis on inclusion as a continually active process is a central part of their definition. They see inclusion as a continuous process of reflection and review rather than being an end product. Other writers have also stressed this point (Ainscow *et al.*, 1999). This is a logical argument given the fact that schools will continually have to review their policies and practices in order to meet the needs of an ever-changing population of pupils. Corbett (2001, 1) refers to a *connective pedagogy*, which connects the learner with their own way of learning, thus connecting them with the curriculum. She emphasises that *where a school community is sensitive to its sub-cultures and gives them value and respect, it is an inclusive community* (Corbett, 2001,12).

A SUMMARY OF **KEY POINTS**

> **Inclusive education reflects a commitment to all children. It is not just about children with special educational needs.**

> **An inclusive education system demands a radical transformation of the curriculum and assessment systems so that success can be measured in many different ways. Measuring children against norm-related standards is not inclusive, as this system produces winners and losers.**

> **All teachers need to take seriously their responsibility for the education of all children.**

MOVING *ON* > > > > > > MOVING *ON* > > > > > > MOVING *ON*

Consider ways in which you can be more inclusive in your teaching of children with special needs on your next placement.

REFERENCES REFERENCES **REFERENCES** REFERENCES **REFERENCES** REFERENCES

Ainscow, M., Farrell, P., Tweddle, D. and Malki, G. (1999) 'The role of LEA's in developing inclusive policies and practices', *British Journal of Special Education*, 26 (3), 136–140.

Allan, J. (2003), 'Productive pedagogies and the challenge of inclusion', *British Journal of Special Education,* 30 (4), 175–179.

Armstrong, D. (1998), Changing faces, changing places: Policy routes to inclusion, in P. Clough and L. Barton (eds), *Managing Inclusive Education: From Policy to Experience*, London: Paul Chapman Publishing.

Armstrong, D. (2005) 'Reinventing "inclusion": New Labour and the cultural politics of special education', *Oxford Review of Education*, 31 (1), 135–151.

Audit Commission (2002) Special educational needs: A mainstream issue, London: Audit Commission, in Weddell, K. (2005) 'Dilemmas in the Quest for Inclusion', *NASEN*, 32 (1), 3–11.

Barton, L. (1998) 'Markets, managerialism and inclusive education' in P. Clough and L. Barton (eds), (1998) *Managing inclusive education: From policy to experience*. London: Paul Chapman Publishing.

Barton, L. (2003) *Inclusive Education and Teacher Education: A Basis for Hope or a Discourse of Delusion?* London: Institute of Education

Booth, T, Ainscow, M., Black-Hawkins, K., Vaughan, M., and Shaw, L. (2000) *Index for Inclusion*. Bristol: Centre for Studies on Inclusive Education.

Booth, T., Nes, K. and Stromstad, M. (eds) (2003) *Developing Inclusive Teacher Education*. London: Routledge Falmer.

Carrington, S. and Elkins, J. (2005) 'Comparisons of a traditional and an inclusive secondary school culture', in Rix, J., Simmons, K., Nind, M. and Sheehy, K., *Policy and Power in Inclusive Education: Values into Practice*, London: Routledge Falmer/Open University Press.

Cole, B. (2005) 'Good faith and effort? Perspectives on educational inclusion', *Disability and Society*, 20 (3), 331–344.

Corbett, J. (1999) 'Inclusivity and school culture: The case of special education', in J. Prosser (ed), *School Culture*. London: Paul Chapman.

Corbett, J. (2001) 'Teaching approaches which support inclusive education: A connective pedagogy', *British Journal of Special Education*, 28 (2), 55–59.

Corbett, J. and Slee, R. (2000) 'An international conversation on inclusive education', in F. Armstrong, D. Armstrong and L. Barton (eds) *Inclusive Education: Policy Contexts and Comparative Perspectives*. London: David Fulton.

Department for Education and Employment (1997) *Excellence in Schools*, London: Department for Education and Employment.

Department for Education and Employment (DfEE) (1998) *The learning age: A renaissance for a new Britain.* London: HMSO.

Department for Education and Skills (2004) *Removing Barriers to Achievement: The Government Strategy for SEN*. Nottingham: DFES.

Dyson, A. (1997) 'Inclusion: What to include?' Education Review, in Knight, B. (1999) 'Towards inclusion of students with special educational needs in the regular classroom', *NASEN*, 14 (1), 3–7.

Farrell, P. (1997) 'The integration of children with severe learning difficulties: A review of the recent literature', *Journal of Applied Research in Intellectual Disabilities*, 10, 1–14.

Farrell, M. (1998) 'The role of the special educational needs coordinator: Looking forward', *Support for Learning*, 13 (2), 82–86.

Farrell, P. (2001) 'Special education in the last twenty years: Have things really got better?', *British Journal of Special Education*, 28 (1), 3–9.

Farrell, P., Balshaw, M. and Polat, F. (1999) *The Management, Role and Training of Learning Support Assistants*. London: Department for Education and Employment.

Feiler, A. and Gibson, H. (1999) 'Threats to the inclusive movement', *British Journal of Special Education*, 26 (3), 147–152.

Florian, L. (1998) 'An examination of the practical problems associated with the implementation of inclusive education policies', *Support for Learning*, 13 (3), 105–108.

Fulcher, G. (1999) *Disabling Policies? A Comparative Approach to Education Policy and Disability*. Sheffield: Philip Armstrong Publications.

Garner, P. (2001), Goodbye Mr. Chips: Special needs, inclusive education and the deceit of initial teacher training, in T. O'Brian (ed), *Enabling Inclusion: Blue Skies . . . Dark Clouds?*, London: The Stationery Office.

Gewirtz, S., Ball, S. and Bowe, R. (1995), *Markets, Choice and Equity in Education*. Buckingham: Open University Press.

Goodley, D (2007) 'Towards socially just pedagogies: Deleuzoguattarian critical disability studies', *International Journal of Inclusive Education*, 11(3), 319.

Hegarty, S. (1993), 'Reviewing the literature on integration', *European Journal of Special Needs Education,* 8, 194–200.

Hornby, G., Atkinson, M. and Howard, J. (1997) *Controversial Issues in Special Education*. London: David Fulton.

Howe, K.R. and Welner, K.G. (2005) 'School choice and the pressure to perform: Déjà vu for children with disabilities', in Rix, J., Simmons, K., Nind, M., and Sheehy, K., (2005), *Policy and Power in Inclusive Education: Values into Practice*. London: Routledge Falmer/Open University Press.

Hunt, P. and Goetz, L. (1997) 'Research on inclusive educational programs, practices and outcomes for students with severe disabilities. *Journal of Special Education,* 31, 3–29.

Jones, P. (2002) 'Promoting inclusive practices in primary initial teacher training: influencing hearts as well as minds', *Support for Learning,* 17 (20), 58–63.

Knight, B. (1999) 'Towards inclusion of students with special educational needs in the regular classroom', *NASEN,* 14 (1), 3–7.

Lewis, A. (1995) *Children's Understanding of Disability*. London: Routledge.

MacLeod, F. (2001) 'Towards inclusion – Our shared responsibility for disaffected pupils', *British Journal of Special Education,* 28 (4), 191–194.

Mansett, G. and Semmel, M. (1997) 'Are inclusive programs for students with mild disabilities effective? A comparative review of model programs', *Journal of Special Education,* 31, 155–180.

Minke, K.M., Bear, G., Deemer, S.A. and Griffin, S.M. (1996) 'Teachers' experiences with inclusive classrooms: implications for special education reform', *Journal of Special Education,* 30 (2), 152–186.

Poulou, M., and Norwich, B. (2000) 'Teachers' perceptions of students with emotional and behavioural difficulties: Severity and prevalence', *European Journal of special Needs Education,* 15 (2), 171–187.

Riddick, B. (1995) 'Dyslexia: Dispelling the myths', *Disability and Society,* 10 (4), 457–473.

Ring, M.M. and Reetz, L. (2000) 'Modification effects on attributions of middle school students with learning disabilities', *Learning Disabilities Research and Practice,* 15 (1), 34–42.

Rose, R. (2001) 'Primary school teacher perceptions of the conditions required to include pupils with special educational needs, *Educational Review,* 53 (2), 147–156.

Rose, R. and Shelvin, M. (2004) 'Marginalised young people: Encouraging voices: Listening to young people who have been marginalised', *Support for Learning,* 19 (4), 155–161.

Slee, R. (1996) 'Inclusive schooling in Australia? Not yet', *Journal of Education,* 26 (1), 19–32.

Slee, R. (2001) 'Inclusion in practice: Does practice make perfect?', *Educational Review,* 53 (2), 113–123.

Slee, R. and Allan, J. (2001) 'Excluding the included: A reconsideration of inclusive education', *International Studies in Sociology of Education,* 11 (2), 173–191.

Slee, R. and Allan, J. (2005) Excluding the included: A reconsideration of inclusive education, in Rix, J., Simmons, K., Nind, M. and Sheehy, K., *Policy and Power in Inclusive Education: Values into Practice*. London: Routledge Falmer/Open University Press.

Thomas, G. and Loxley, A. (2001) *Deconstructing Special Education and Constructing Inclusion.* Buckingham: Open University Press.

Tregaskis, C. (2002) 'Social model theory: the story so far . . .', *Disability and Society,* 17 (4), 457–470.

Vidovitch, L. and Slee, R. (2001) 'Bringing universities to account? Exploring some global and local policy tensions', *Journal of Educational Policy,* 16 (5), 431–453.

Warnock, M. (1996) 'The work of the Warnock Committee', in P. Mittler and V. Sinason (eds) *Changing Policy and Practice for People with Learning Difficulties*. London: Castle.

Warnock, M. (2005) *Special Educational Needs: A New Look,* Impact No.11, Philosophy of Education Society of Great Britain.

Wedell, K. (2005) 'Dilemmas in the quest for inclusion', *British Journal of Special Education,* 32 (1), 3–11.

Winter, E.C. (2006) 'Preparing new teachers for inclusive schools and classrooms', *Support for Learning,* 21 (2), 85–91.

FURTHER READING FURTHER READING **FURTHER READING** FURTHER READING

Allan, J. (1996) 'Foucault and special educational needs: A "box of tools" for analysing children's experiences of mainstreaming', *Disability and Society*, 11 (2), 219–233.

In this article Allan applies Foucault's theoretical framework to inclusive education. She simplifies Foucault's work and uses his framework to analyse inclusive education.

Useful website

Centre for Studies on Inclusive Education
http://inclusion.uwe.ac.uk/csie/csiehome.htm
This website has a wealth of information about inclusive education.

2
The Special Educational Needs Code of Practice

Chapter objectives

By the end of this chapter you should be aware of the:

- **key principles of the Code of Practice for Special Educational Needs and the implications of these for teachers;**
- **implications of the Disability Discrimination Act for teachers;**
- **importance of Individual Education Plans;**
- **'graduated response' to special educational needs.**

This chapter addresses the following Professional Standards for the award of QTS:

Q3(a), Q4, Q5, Q6, Q19, Q20

Introduction

This chapter introduces you to the key principles of the Code of Practice for Special Educational Needs and the implication of this document for you as a teacher. It is important that you clearly understand the statutory framework within which teachers work (QTS Standard 3a) and the overarching agendas and policy documents which will ultimately shape your classroom practice. This chapter provides an overview of the key aspects of the Code of Practice as well as making links to key legislation and policy agendas which have been influenced by the Code. We draw on examples of case studies from practice to illustrate key points and practical tasks extend your learning further.

Key principles of the Code of Practice

The current SEN Code of Practice (DfES, 2001) has been effective since 2001. The Code is underpinned with several fundamental principles listed below.

- A child with special educational needs should have their needs met.
- The special educational needs of children should normally be met in mainstream provision.
- The views of children should be sought and taken into account.
- Parents and those with parental responsibility play a crucial role in supporting their child's education.
- Children with Special Educational Needs are entitled to full access to a broad, balanced and relevant education.

(DfES, 2001, 1: 5: 7)

The current Code of Practice replaces the 1994 Code of Practice, which was a consequence of the 1993 Education Act. While the Code is not enshrined in statute law, the document explicitly states that *LEAs, schools, early education settings and those who help them must have regard to it. They must not ignore it* (DfES, 2001, iii). The revised Code extended the rights of parents to have their views taken into account. In addition it also emphasises the rights of children to express their views and have their opinion taken into account.

The Code of Practice identifies several *critical success factors* (DfES, 2001, 1: 6: 1) which follow on from the key principles described above. These include the need for professionals to: identify children's needs early; establish effective partnerships with pupils and parents; review interventions regularly; work within a multidisciplinary framework; and work within prescribed time limits. The Code clearly emphasises the importance of schools working in partnership with pupils, parents and other agencies and the principles of working in partnership and multidisciplinary approaches to practice were subsequently reflected in the *Every Child Matters* agenda.

As a trainee teacher it is likely that you will be working with children who have been identified as having special educational needs. You will need to develop effective partnerships with parents and carers under the guidance of your teacher-mentor. You will need to think carefully about ways in which you can actively seek the views of parents and you will need to consider ways in which parents can support the learning that takes place inside your classroom. This may be a daunting task at first but you will develop in confidence as you gain more practical experience during your course.

Firstly, it will be necessary for you to reflect on your own values and beliefs about genuine partnership working. For example, to what extent do you believe that parents have a crucial role to play in raising standards (see QTS Standard Q5) and how far do you think they should be involved in the decision-making process? You will need to communicate effectively with parents and carers (see Standard Q4) and maintain a commitment to collaborative working practices (see Standard Q6). You will need to think carefully about how you actively seek the perspectives of pupils. Current thinking emphasises the rights of pupils to participate in the setting of learning targets and to be involved in other decisions relating to their education. You may need to reconsider your own values in relation to your stance on pupils' rights to express their opinion, their rights to have their opinion heard and acted upon and their rights to shape their curriculum. We use the word 'rights' here to emphasise that these are key entitlements under the Code of Practice and *Every Child Matters*. For some trainee teachers, pupil and parent participation will represent a new way of thinking about education, teaching and learning. It will also reflect a less hierarchical and more equal relationship with key stakeholders.

It has been argued that *the Code's explicit endorsement of the principle of a common curriculum for all marks a new policy development in the field of special needs education* (Skidmore, 2004, 13). However, one might question whether the programmes of study in the current National Curriculum and the associated level descriptors are appropriate and relevant to children with special educational needs. For example, the level descriptors fail to acknowledge the small steps that many children with special needs take. These steps are significant and are worthy of acknowledgement. The P-levels are more useful for tracking progress as they identify smaller steps that children with SEN progress through.

Cole (2005) talks about the 'risks' involved with educating children with SEN: there is a risk that children with SEN may be experiencing bullying in mainstream schools; there is a risk that the presence of many children with SEN in mainstream schools may have a detrimental effect on school performance indicators and there are financial and political risks (Cole, 2005). However, Cole stresses that the risks are worth taking and that as a society we should *be willing to commit ourselves to the challenge of inclusion; to commit ourselves to 'good faith and effort' in the cause of equity and social justice* (Cole, 2005, 342).

Disability Discrimination Act

The Disability Discrimination Act 2005 places a duty on all public bodies, schools and local authorities to eliminate discrimination and harassment related to disability, promote equality of opportunity and positive attitudes towards disabled people and take steps to take account of the needs of disabled people. In some circumstances this will involve treating disabled people more favourably than other people (TDA, 2008). Under this legislation schools and local authorities have a duty to develop a disability equality scheme. The legislation requires all schools and Early Years settings to make 'reasonable adjustments' to policies and practices in order to ensure equality of opportunity.

The procedures set out in the Code of Practice enable you to demonstrate how you have made reasonable adjustments to enable you to cater for the needs of learners with disabilities. You will be required to document the additional and different strategies you have used to support your learners. The procedures in the Code of Practice enable you to demonstrate how you have adjusted your planning and teaching strategies to meet the needs of specific learners. They enable you to document the specific access strategies you have built into your practice to enable learners with disabilities to participate fully in the curriculum and the social life of the school. The duty to make reasonable adjustments extends to all aspects of school life, including educational visits.

CASE STUDY

Reasonable adjustments

Khalid was four years old when he entered Reception class with a statement of special educational needs. Transition meetings with the nursery staff had taken place. The Reception teacher had also visited Khalid to observe and work with him in the nursery prior to transition. It became evident that Khalid had been excluded from the nursery on several occasions due to his inappropriate and disruptive behaviour. The nursery practitioners considered his behaviour to be high-risk in terms of the safety of other children.

Khalid entered the Reception class and immediately challenged the expectations and routines of the setting. The practitioner had considered clear, focused and appropriate expectations for Khalid. These were conveyed to him and consistently reiterated. It became evident that Khalid enjoyed playing to the audience. Incidences of inappropriate behaviour resulted in Khalid being accompanied to a safe 'thinking space' away from the gaze of adults and other children. Here his inappropriate behaviour and reasons for withdrawal were explained to Khalid. Further conversation was terminated at this point and the accompanying practitioner ignored any ensuing outbursts. Initially Khalid responded by shouting, throwing chairs and biting and these episodes were initially very prolonged. Once Khalid had calmed, the practitioner resumed a dialogue with him, and asked if he understood why it had been necessary for him to leave the setting. Initially Khalid could not respond and a simple explanation was given to him. Over time Khalid was given the opportunity to explain and discuss his feelings and reasons for his behaviour. He was told that he could return to the setting but if there was a repeat of his inappropriate behaviour he would again leave the setting. Khalid initially challenged these expectations and it was therefore essential that the practitioner was consistent in her approach. Over several weeks Khalid spent less time in the 'thinking space' and when it became necessary to take him there his outbursts lasted for shorter periods of time. Interestingly, over several months Khalid took ownership of the 'thinking space' and would ask to go to it whenever he felt agitated.

- What reasonable adjustments did the practitioner implement to enable her to manage and support Khalid?
- How did the practitioner give Khalid a voice?
- How did the reasonable adjustment become a tool for both the practitioner and the child?

Removing barriers to achievement

Removing barriers to achievement (DfES, 2004) is the government's strategy for SEN. This strategy encapsulates the principles of the Code of Practice and the *Every Child Matters* agenda. The strategy outlines the government's key principles for SEN. These are:

- early intervention;
- removing barriers to learning;
- raising expectations and achievement;
- delivering improvements in partnership.

The strategy also embraces the principles of the statutory framework for inclusion in the National Curriculum (DfEE, 1999), which emphasises the need for schools to develop inclusive practices through the identification and removal of barriers to learning.

As a trainee teacher you need therefore to develop positive attitudes towards all children. You will need to be committed to the notion of personalised learning for individual pupils and you will need to have high expectations of all children. When planning lessons it is important that you think carefully about the strategies which you can build into your teaching to enable learners to access the curriculum. For example, a child with dyslexia may find it difficult to read from white paper but a simple coloured overlay might help that child to read better. The access strategies which you use will depend on the specific needs of the child. A child who has a specific difficulty with number recognition might benefit from a simple number square as a reference point. A child with autism might find it easier to access the curriculum through the use of computer-based resources. Access strategies may constitute minor or major adjustments to classroom practice. The key point is that you need to do all you can to enable all learners to access the curriculum. Therefore, inclusion does not mean treating all learners equally. Sometimes children will require different provision to access common learning content and at other times different content will be necessary. It all depends on the specific needs of your learners.

As a teacher you will be able to make an informed decision about whether it is appropriate for the whole class to learn common subject matter. You might be able to build in some access strategies to enable your learners with SEN to access the same curriculum as the rest of the class. At other times you will make a professional decision that aspects of the curriculum may be inappropriate for your learners with SEN and that they require different provision in order to meet their needs. There is no magic recipe as children are all individual and have different needs. The key point is that you have the same high standards for all your learners, taking their starting points into account. You should therefore have an expectation that all learners will make progress and will make steps forward in their learning, however small those steps may be. The steps may be small in comparison to other learners but for a child with SEN small steps could be a major leap forward. You will need to plan for meeting children's next steps in learning and when children successfully achieve these it is important that you instil in them a sense of achievement. You will need to know about early childhood development and have a very clear understanding of children's progression through a specific aspect of learning. The P-scales are a very useful starting point for tracking the progress of learners with SEN in Key Stage 1 and beyond. The age-related targets in the Early Years Foundation Stage framework (DfES, 2007) are a useful reference point for planning children's next steps in the Early Years and early Key Stage 1. If you have a clear understanding of the steps you want your learners to go through, you can then have high expectations and plan for progression in learning.

Armstrong (2005) and Lloyd have questioned the extent to which the government has uncritically applied the standards agenda universally to all children. The Code of Practice provides compensatory measures so that all children achieve the same standards. However, *achievement conceived in this way can be seen to create the greatest barrier to success* (Lloyd, 2008, 229). Current national targets are thus based on *an uncritical view of normality* (Armstrong, 2005, 149). It could therefore be argued that the current national norms need to be critically interrogated for their appropriateness to all learners. This debate opens up the possibility that 'achievement' can be defined in different ways for different learners.

Graduated response

The Code of Practice outlines a graduated response for meeting children's needs. This approach *recognises that there is a continuum of special educational needs* (DfES, 2001, 5: 20: 48) and that some children may eventually require specialist support to enable them to make further progress. However, the Code explicitly states that schools should make use of all internal resources before calling on the support of outside agencies.

The graduated response is a model of action and intervention, designed to support children with special educational needs. In the Early Years sector settings should intervene at Early Years Action and Early Years Action Plus. In the primary phase schools should intervene at School Action and School Action Plus. The Code emphasises that these levels of intervention are not usually steps towards statutory assessment (described below), nor *hurdles to be crossed before a statutory assessment can be made* (DfES, 2001, 5: 22: 48). This model of action is summarised below.

Early Years Action/School Action

At this stage the Special Educational Needs Co-ordinator (SENCO), teacher or practitioner will work in partnership with children and parents to provide interventions that are additional to and different from normal differentiated provision. Teachers and practitioners will need to be alert to children who appear to be making little progress, despite specific, targeted intervention within the specific area of weakness. Children with difficulties in literacy or mathematics or those with persistent emotional and behavioural difficulties, physical or sensory problems or difficulties with communication or interaction, may require support at Early Years/School Action if progress is minimal despite differentiation. The role of the SENCO is to take the lead in further monitoring and assessment. Children at this stage may receive additional support from support staff but this might not always be appropriate and the nature of the intervention will depend on the specific needs of the child. Targeted differentiation or the use of specialist equipment to overcome barriers to learning might constitute reasonable adjustments to the provision at this stage. The strategies adopted or interventions are recorded on an Individual Education Plan (IEP).

REFLECTIVE TASK

In your placement school ask your teacher-mentor for samples of current IEPs. You will need these to inform your planning. Reflect on the set target for individual learners. These should be focused and achievable and additional to and different from the differentiated provision within the class.

- Are the targets focused and achievable?
- Are the targets measurable?
- Are the success criteria clear?
- Could the targets have been met within normal differentiated curriculum planning?

PRACTICAL TASK PRACTICAL TASK PRACTICAL TASK PRACTICAL TASK PRACTICAL TASK

In your placement school take opportunities to work in collaboration with other professionals, parents and the child to review progress against IEP success criteria. You may have the opportunity to discuss and contribute to the setting of new targets. Your contributions will be valued.

Early Years Action Plus/School Action Plus

At Early Years Action Plus/School Action Plus the school or setting will usually enlist the support of external services and agencies to support them in assessing the needs of the child and making provision for these needs. The local authority may provide some services to meet the specific needs of children. If children continue to make little or no progress at Early Years Action/School Action or assessments indicate that a child is working at a level considerably below his/her peers, then these could be triggers for Early Years Action Plus/ School Action Plus. Additionally, if a child requires an individualised behaviour management programme or has ongoing and communication difficulties that constitute a substantial barrier to learning, schools and settings may consider intervention at this level. Some children may have sensory or physical needs and therefore require access to specialist services. These triggers for intervention at Early Years Action Plus or School Action Plus are outlined in the Code of Practice (DfES, 2001, 5: 56: 55).

At this stage, external specialists can provide practitioners with advice on teaching strategies and interventions and they can support the school or setting with the assessment process. Parents and carers should be consulted throughout this process.

Practitioners should not assume that slow progress is automatically a result of a deficiency within the child. The social model of disability has been discussed in Chapter 1 and encourages us to conceptualise disability as a social construct. Therefore wider factors such as exposure to appropriate teaching and factors related to school organisation might adversely affect pupils' rates of progress. This is acknowledged in the Code but it has been argued that the norms on which assessments are made *are effectively taken for* granted, and attention is concentrated upon the failings of the individual pupil (Skidmore, 2004, 16). This critique opens up a debate about whether the Code effectively labels children as having special needs on the basis of their failure to meet government-defined norms, milestones and targets. The Code defines measures of 'progress' in terms of the gap between an individual child's attainment and that of their peers. From a critical perspective, the Code fails to acknowledge that these measures of 'normality' may not be appropriate to all children and that different success indicators may be needed for different children. The Code applies the government-defined norms to all children and therefore effectively labels children as being in 'need' of intervention and support.

CASE STUDY
Parental voice

Ben entered his nursery setting at the age of three. The practitioners in the setting noticed that Ben had some speech problems. Ben's speech was limited and he communicated through pointing and the use of isolated words. It was noted that Ben's parents responded to his pointing and use of isolated words and his needs were usually met immediately. Observations had indicated that Ben also had low self-esteem. He quickly became upset if he was asked to complete new activities. The practitioners in the nursery were concerned about Ben's speech development. In consultation with the SENCO and the parents, they decided to place Ben on Early Years Action.

The parents were invited into the setting for a meeting. Their views, experiences and observations of Ben in his home setting were discussed to form a holistic assessment of Ben's achievements and needs. Ben's parents confirmed that they also had concerns related to some aspects of Ben's speech development. At the meeting strategies were discussed and shared to address the immediate concerns. One of the targets agreed at the meeting for Ben's IEP was that Ben's use of pointing and isolated words should be followed by a modelled simple phrase or sentence, which conveyed the same meaning. For example, Ben pointed and said *cat*. The adult modelled this by saying *there's a cat*. The parents were encouraged to share this strategy with immediate family members and all adults who had regular contact with Ben.

REFLECTIVE TASK

- Why was it important for Ben's parents to contribute to his IEP?
- How would you ensure that the parents continued to have a voice?
- What additional targets would have been appropriate to support Ben's development?

Individual Education Plans

The Individual Education Plan (IEP) is a tool for recording:

- the child's short-term targets;
- the teaching strategies to be used;
- the provision to be put in place (intervention);
- when the plan is to be reviewed;

- the success/exit criteria for measuring whether the target(s) have been met;
- the outcomes.

(DfES, 2001, 5: 50: 54)

Essentially the IEP should record provision that is additional to and different from normal differentiated provision. Teachers should record three or four individual targets and these should be focused and measurable. Teachers should always involve parents or carers in setting and reviewing targets. The Code recommends that IEPs should be reviewed twice a year. The views of parents should be sought at the review point and the SENCO should be involved in the monitoring and review process. The Code recommends that where possible, children *should be consulted as part of the review process* (DfES, 2001, 5: 53: 54).

According to Skidmore, the IEP *owes much to an objectives-based model of teaching inspired ultimately by theories of learning derived from behavioural psychology* (Skidmore, 2004, 16). He emphasises that individualised approaches such as these *may act as a straightjacket* [sic] *upon more creative, innovative approaches to provision* (Skidmore, 2004, 16). The implications of Skidmore's critique are worthy of consideration. Teachers need to embrace creative pedagogical approaches for all children. Innovative approaches to teaching and learning are more likely to motivate all learners. Intervention programmes to support learning are often identified on IEPs as strategies for raising attainment. Teachers and trainee teachers should critically examine these carefully to check that they are relevant and engaging for learners with special educational needs.

When you are on placement you will need to find out if any children in your class have an IEP. Ask your teacher-mentor for a copy of the IEPs and look carefully at the targets set for individual pupils. Think carefully about how you might address these targets. Some strategies for addressing the targets will already be documented on the IEP but you might have your own ideas as well and these should be shared with your teacher-mentor and parents, if possible. If an IEP review is planned to take place during your placement, ask if you can take part in the review as a silent observer. We recommend this, particularly if it is your first teaching placement. As you gain further experience during your course you might feel confident enough to join in the discussion. Try to keep parents and carers informed about pupils' progress towards meeting the targets and make sure that you have regular discussions with the pupils about their progress towards their targets. You might need to keep reminding some children about their targets and therefore you would be wise to devise systems for communicating individual targets to children.

Statutory assessment

This process enables local authorities to consider whether a child with special educational needs requires additional provision. According to the Code of Practice, the needs of the majority of learners will be met effectively through Early Years and School Action and Early Years Action Plus and School Action Plus (DfES, 2001). The Code is explicit in stating that the need for a statutory assessment will only apply to *a very small number of cases* (p74).

During statutory assessment the local authority will work in collaboration with the school, the child's parents and other agencies to determine whether a statutory assessment is necessary and a decision to undertake a statutory assessment will not automatically result in a statement of special educational needs. The school, parent or other agency may request a referral for statutory assessment.

Clear evidence needs to be provided to support a referral for a statutory assessment. This should include evidence of intervention and progress over time, reports and assessments from external agencies, the views of parents and the child. Schools will be required to demonstrate that they have followed the advice of other professionals with specialist knowledge. Requests for statutory assessment may be turned down if insufficient evidence is available. Therefore you will need to be rigorous and efficient in keeping dated records of intervention and assessment. In some cases the local authority will conclude that intervention at Early Years Action Plus or School Action Plus is appropriate or they might suggest alternative ways of working with the child (DfES, 2001). Schools must consult parents before requesting a statutory assessment. Clear time limits are stipulated to ensure that the process is carried out in a timely manner.

PRACTICAL TASK PRACTICAL TASK **PRACTICAL TASK** PRACTICAL TASK **PRACTICAL TASK**

During your school-based placement there may be an opportunity for you to be a silent observer during a review meeting for a specific child. This might be an IEP review meeting or an annual review for a child with a statutory assessment. This will present you with a valuable opportunity to observe the way in which professionals from different agencies work collaboratively. After the meeting consider the way in which the meeting was structured and the ways in which the contributions of different agencies acknowledged the child's achievements and identified the areas for future support.

Developing partnerships with parents and carers

According to Skidmore (2004, 13), the Code *considerably extended and strengthened* the rights of parents through the introduction of Local Authority Parent Partnership Services and the Independent Parental Supporter. These will be discussed further in Chapter 8. As a trainee teacher you are required to develop effective partnerships with parents before you are allowed to qualify. You should communicate effectively with parents by using accessible language, free from educational jargon.

It is important that you form effective partnerships with the parents or carers of all the children in your class. However, it is particularly important that you actively seek the views of parents and carers of children with SEN. The Code stresses that parents *hold key information and have a critical role to play in their children's education* (DfES, 2001, 2: 2: 16). The Code outlines the entitlement of parents and carers to have access to information, advice and support during assessment and decision-making processes as well as their entitlement to express their views about how their child is educated. Teachers should be sensitive to the *emotional investment* (DfES, 2001, 2: 7: 17) of parents and take their feelings into account. The experience of rearing a child with special educational needs can be hugely rewarding, but it may also produce feelings of anxiety. As a trainee teacher you should focus on the significant achievements of children with special needs and you should communicate these to parents on a regular basis. Try to develop a genuine partnership where both parties respect the views of each other. Avoid being confrontational, especially in the case of children with social, emotional and behavioural difficulties. You should take seriously parental anxieties and strive to act on these. A simple strategy, such as noting down parental concerns in a meeting with parents, may be all that is required to show them that their views matter.

Soan (2005) reminds trainees to reflect on their own value judgements and to steer clear of stereotypical assumptions about parenting styles and children's upbringing. Undoubtedly, prejudices and stereotypes can influence the way we work with different people. In teaching there is no room for this type of discrimination. All parents deserve an equal amount of time and they all have a right to express their opinion, to be listened to and to have their opinions acted upon. In short, they need to feel that you are doing your very best for their child and that you understand their anxieties.

Listening to pupil voice: developing partnerships with pupils

Skidmore (2004, 15) states that *the revised Code places a stronger emphasis on pupil participation than its predecessor*. The notion of pupil participation is discussed in more detail in Chapter 8. However, it is also briefly introduced here to illustrate its centrality in the Code of Practice. The Code of Practice stresses that:

> *Children and young people with special educational needs have a unique knowledge of their own needs and circumstances and their own views about what sort of help they would like to help them make the most of their education. They should, where possible, participate in all the decision-making processes that occur in education.*

> (DfES, 2001, 3:2:27)

Teachers should therefore consult with children about their learning targets and take active steps to involve them in decisions about their learning. Pupils should contribute, where possible, to their IEPs and be fully involved in any reviews of their progress. Additionally, teachers should involve children in planning the curriculum and consult them about their interests. Effective teachers are able to shape the curriculum around the interests and needs of learners.

For some trainees, this way of working will be in stark contrast to their own educational experiences. It might be interesting for you to think back to your own experiences as a learner in primary school. How often were you consulted about your learning targets? How often were you provided with opportunities to shape your own curriculum? Were you allowed to attend consultation meetings where your progress was discussed? The Code recognises that the emphasis on pupil participation has associated challenges. For example, it might be more difficult to seek the views of very young children or those with severe communication difficulties (DfES, 2001, 3:3:27). These challenges are discussed further in Chapter 8. During your teaching placements you should think carefully about how you are going to develop pupil participation for all learners, not just those with SEN. Think of ways to consult with pupils about what they want to learn and try to build your curriculum plan around their interests. If you have children in your class with social, emotional and behavioural difficulties you will need to consult with them regularly about the strategies that might be implemented in order to help manage their behaviour. Regular consultation with pupils minimises the power relationship between teachers and pupils and this can foster productive relationships with pupils.

Developing effective partnerships with colleagues

The professional standards for QTS identify the need for all trainee teachers to work effectively in collaboration with other colleagues. What are the implications of this for the education of learners with SEN?

Many of you will experience working in partnership with teaching assistants and other support staff when you undertake placements. It is really important that you think carefully about how you deploy these staff in your lessons. In some lessons learners with SEN can be supported by an adult within a group context. The adult could break the task(s) down further or build in strategies to enable specific children to access learning outcomes for the group task(s). At other times, it may be appropriate for children with SEN work on a one-to-one basis with an adult, especially if they need to work on specific targets identified on their IEP. You will need to be cautious about the overuse of targeted one-to-one support as this in itself can become a barrier to learning and could be deemed to be exclusionary. It is a question of balance. You also need to ensure that learners with SEN have input from a teacher at times. As a trainee teacher you need to know all of your pupils. In our professional experience too many children with SEN are not taught by their teachers. We have witnessed them being taught exclusively by support staff and often this takes place outside of classrooms. Classroom assistants can be invaluable in helping you to develop a more inclusive classroom. However, the ineffective deployment of support staff can be a barrier to inclusion.

Think carefully about how you capitalise on the support you have in your classroom. Do you deploy your classroom assistant(s) to support learning during lesson introductions and plenaries? Do you plan to meet the needs of learners with SEN in collaboration with support staff? Do you involve support staff in the assessment of pupils' learning? Effective teamwork demands greater effort than merely getting along with each other and being polite. It is about sharing knowledge and skills across the team. If you involve your classroom assistant in the planning and assessment process, s/he is more likely to feel valued and you will be able to problem-solve and work out solutions together. Very often, support staff have a deep knowledge of the learners they are working with and you need to tap into this to enable you to plan effectively.

It is important that you meet regularly with the SENCO to keep them informed about the progress of specific learners and to provide them with opportunities to share their expertise with you about working with learners with SEN. In addition, find the time to talk to teaching colleagues about specific learners. It is likely that they may have knowledge of the learners you are working with and they may be able to help you in developing strategies for your learners.

Remember that there are a range of services and agencies in the local authority and professionals that work for these services may already have some involvement with individual children. For example, some children may be supported by the educational psychology service, the behavioural support service or other services such as speech and language therapy or the communication and interaction team. Staff from these services may come into school to advise teachers and to carry out assessments on individual children. As a trainee teacher, try to find time to speak to these colleagues and ask them for advice if you need support. You are not expected to have specialist knowledge of SEN at this stage of your career, or even as a classroom teacher, but you are expected to work in collaboration with other colleagues. Working effectively with colleagues will make the job more enjoyable and rewarding and will be of greater benefit to all learners.

Working in partnership with other agencies

The *Every Child Matters* agenda stresses the importance of effective multidisciplinary working practices to meet the needs of specific learners. The Code of Practice (DfES, 2001, 135) emphasises the need for a *seamless* service with the aim of providing *integrated, high quality, holistic support focused on the needs of the child*. Different agencies involved in supporting the child therefore need to work collaboratively to ensure early identification and focused intervention, working in partnership with parents and the child.

You do not have to work in isolation to meet the needs of children with special educational needs. Some of these needs will be complex and challenging and lie outside the realms of your own professional knowledge. Such services include the following but this is not an exhaustive list.

- Visual and hearing-impaired support services.
- Educational psychologists.
- Behaviour support services.
- Counsellors.
- Speech and language therapists.
- Cognition and learning support services.
- Communication and interaction teams.
- Education welfare service.

PRACTICAL TASK PRACTICAL TASK PRACTICAL TASK PRACTICAL TASK PRACTICAL TASK

During your school-based placement identify opportunities to further your understanding of the roles and responsibilities of different professionals in supporting children with special educational needs. These may include educational psychologists, the SENCO, speech and language therapists, behaviour specialists, physiotherapists, visual and hearing-impaired specialists or professionals from a communication and interaction team. This is not an exhaustive list. Some of these professionals may well be supporting children and practitioners in your placement setting. It would be useful to arrange a mutually convenient time to discuss their roles. Additionally you may wish to 'shadow' them as they work with children and other professionals in your school. Following your experience of shadowing multi-agency professionals, carefully consider the ways in which this expertise is disseminated to school-based professionals and the ways in which reasonable adjustments are made to adopt the advice given.

REFLECTIVE TASK

Every Child Matters strongly promotes the expectations and value of multi-agency work. In your experience, what do you think are the facilitators and barriers to multi-agency work? Discuss this with a colleague.

RESEARCH SUMMARY RESEARCH SUMMARY **RESEARCH SUMMARY** RESEARCH SUMMARY

Armstrong, D. (2005) 'Reinventing "inclusion": New Labour and the cultural politics of special education', *Oxford Review of Education,* 31 (1), 135–151.

In this article Armstrong draws together a critique of the Code of Practice and the issues associated with the government's conceptualisation of inclusion. This article will enable you to critically analyse the inclusion agenda and will provide a critical basis for formulating a critical discussion for an assignment on inclusive education.

A SUMMARY OF **KEY POINTS**

> The Code of Practice emphasises the importance of the voice of the child, parents and carers in planning and decision-making processes.

> The Disability Discrimination Act 2005 places a duty on schools to make reasonable adjustments to cater for the needs of children with disabilities.

> Individual Education Plans allow teachers to record individual targets which are focused and measurable.

> The graduated response encompasses intervention at School Action, School Action Plus and Statutory Assessment.

MOVING *ON* > > > > > > **MOVING** *ON* > > > > > > **MOVING** *ON*

Now that you understand the principles of the Code of Practice, you now need to become confident with using pupils' IEP targets to inform the planning process. When you are next on placement it will be useful if you can collect copies of the IEPs for children in your class. Discuss the targets with your mentor and discuss ways in which you can take account of these targets when planning lessons.

REFERENCES REFERENCES **REFERENCES** REFERENCES **REFERENCES** REFERENCES

Armstrong, D. (2005) 'Reinventing "Inclusion": New Labour and the cultural politics of special education, *Oxford Review of Education*, 31 (1), 135–151.

Cole, B.A. (2005) '"Good faith and effort?" Perspectives on educational inclusion', *Disability and Society*, 20 (3), 331–344.

Lloyd, C. (2008) 'Removing barriers to achievement: a strategy for inclusion or exclusion?', *International Journal of inclusive Education*, 12 (2), 221–236.

DfEE (1999) *The National Curriculum for England*. London: DfEE.

DfES (2001) *Special Educational Needs Code of Practice*. Nottingham: DfES.

DfES (2004) *Removing Barriers to Achievement: the Government's strategy for SEN*. Nottingham: DfES.

DfES (2007) *The Early Years Foundation Stage: Setting the standards for learning, development and care for children from birth to five*. Nottingham: DfES.

Skidmore, D. (2004) *Inclusion: the dynamic of school development*. Berkshire: Open University Press.

Soan, S. (2005) *Reflective reader: Primary special educational needs*. Exeter: Learning Matters.

TDA (2008) *Special educational needs and/or disabilities: A training resource for initial teacher training providers: primary undergraduate courses*. London: TDA.

FURTHER READING FURTHER READING **FURTHER READING** FURTHER READING

Soan, S. (2005) *Reflective reader: Primary special educational needs*. Exeter: Learning Matters.
  This is a very useful text because it takes the reader through all the key principles of the Code of Practice, as well as covering key legislation.

Useful website

www.sentrain.net/sencode/index.asp

3
Learning and cognition

Chapter objectives

This chapter will enable you to:

- recognise the range of needs associated with learning and cognition;
- understand the terminology used to define these needs;
- recognise some of the generic support needs of children with learning difficulties;
- consider some teaching styles and strategies that can be adopted to assist children with learning difficulties;
- understand how these can help a child to process and record information effectively.

This chapter addresses the following Professional Standards for the award of QTS:

Q10, Q19, Q25a, Q25b, Q25c, Q25d, Q26b, Q29

Introduction

The Oxford Dictionary defines learning as *The act, process, or experience of gaining knowledge or skill. Knowledge or skill gained through schooling or study.*

Critics of the way in which many educators have approached learning in the past include Claxton (2008), who argues that our school system is based on a nineteenth-century industrial model which relied upon a content-driven curriculum where being competent at passing examinations such as the eleven-plus was seen as the passport to success. At this time intelligence was defined as the capacity of an individual to demonstrate rational thought and translate this into clear logical speech and writing. While these elements are important, the work of Howard Gardner on what he describes as 'multiple intelligences' opens up a much wider profile. Gardner (1983) says that we all possess a set of different intelligence strengths which we use and apply to learn. These 'intelligences' include linguistic, physical, mathematical and many others. How and when we use them determines how we understand new ideas. Different cultures also view different 'intelligences' highly.

There is no doubt that our views on learning have evolved since the nineteenth century and continue to do so, as evidenced by both the recent reviews of the primary curriculum.

The Rose review of the primary curriculum (2009) states:

> The touchstone of an excellent curriculum is that it instills [sic] *in children a love of learning for its own sake. This means that primary children must not only learn what to study, they must also learn how to study, and thus become confident, self-disciplined individuals capable of engaging a lifelong process of learning.*

The Cambridge Primary Review (2009) states as one of its aims that learning should:

> *excite, promote and sustain children's agency, empowering them through knowledge, understanding, skill and personal qualities to profit from their learning,*

to discover and lead rewarding lives, and to manage life and find new meaning in a changing world.

Cognitive development

The importance of cognitive development to SEN is central in that an inability to function in the cognitive domain is fundamentally linked to learning difficulties.

(Garner, 2009)

Cognition is the acquisition, storage, retrieval and use of knowledge. It is the ability of the brain to think, process and store information and to solve problems. It follows that cognition is fundamental to learning. There are several different ways of describing cognitive development and some of these are outlined below. Our understanding of cognitive development began with the work of Jean Piaget at the beginning of the twentieth century. Before this time psychologists such as Freud, Pavlov, Watson and Skinner had concentrated their attention more upon behaviour as the vehicle for learning. Behaviourist theory relies upon observed behaviours and discounts mental activity. For this reason we will concentrate upon cognitive psychology in this chapter.

Piaget, the Swiss philosopher, sociologist and psychologist, began studying how we acquire knowledge and understanding of the world. His interpretation of cognitive development differs from that of others in that he sees the child as a 'lone scientist' individually exploring the world and individually assimilating new information and accommodating to new experience (Jarvis, 2005). He identified four stages of logical development which he called operations. He called these operations sensorimotor, preoperational, concrete operational and formal operational, and broadly described them in the following way.

Sensorimotor (0–2 years)

Children have no symbolic thought or operations and are operating at a prelogical stage. Children interpret the world through physical sensation, learning to associate actions by trial and error. They are very egocentric. By the end of this stage children have usually acquired some language and can think using words.

Preoperational (2–7 years)

There is symbolic thought but no operations. They still see the world very much as it appears to them, remain egocentric and have still to grasp logical rules or operations, being able to focus on only one aspect at a time. For example, if shown a short, fat container and a long thin vessel containing equal amounts of water they will identify the tall vessel as containing the most water. Once they can recognise that the two vessels contain an equal volume of water they are moving on to the stage of concrete operations. Piaget described this as conservation. Similarly, at this stage they do not discriminate between living and non-living things, often attributing lifelike characteristics to inanimate objects. Piaget called this animism.

Concrete operational (7–11 years)

The child can deal with physical objects and conserve information. There is a tendency to lose the animism aspect and to be less egocentric. They retain the need for physical objects to help them to carry out logical tasks.

Formal operational (>11 years)

Children can think in abstract concepts and devise and test hypotheses. They are capable of formulating a system of values and ideals.

Piagetian theory determines that teaching has to be pitched at the level of the stage within which the child is operating as an individual. It follows that a child with a learning difficulty may be operating within a different stage to their chronological age. There is some debate about whether Piaget underestimates the abilities of children in the reasoning abilities of young children and overestimates those of older children (Jarvis, 2005).

Social constructivism

Piaget's idea formed the basis of subsequent study but relegated adults to unobtrusive helpers (Penn, 2008). While his ideas are still highly regarded, our understanding of cognitive development has progressed. The work of social constructivists such as Vygotsky, Brunner and Gardner has widely expanded our thinking about cognition.

Although Lev Vygotsky was a contemporary of Piaget, his work did not come to world renown until the 1970s when his work was translated from Russian. While Piaget regarded play as a kind of scientific rehearsal and thought that children would grow out of it once they had mastered abstract thinking, Vygotsky defined play differently, seeing play as a mental support system which allows children to represent their everyday social reality (Penn, 2008). He saw play as an opportunity for children to construct their learning from the experiences they gained from their surroundings. He wrote: *In play a child is always above his average age, above his daily behaviour; in play it is as though he were a head taller than himself* (1978, 102). Vygotsky coined the phrase the 'zone of proximal development' (ZPD). The zone of proximal development is a theoretical space of understanding which is just beyond the level of understanding of an individual and leads to the area of understanding into which a learner will develop next. Sewell (1990) explains this as *a point at which a child has partly mastered a skill but can act more effectively with the assistance of a more skilled adult or peer*. The implications for a child with learning difficulties are that this may take considerably more repetition to achieve mastery than might be expected for a child who is learning within age expectations. In social constructivism, language is given a high priority and dialogue becomes the medium through which ideas are considered, shared and developed. This dialogue will usually be with a more knowledgeable other who, in practice, is most likely a teacher, parent, other adult family member and occasionally a peer. The knowledgeable other uses dialogue to support the development of understanding. This process, commonly referred to as 'scaffolding', was originally put forward by Wood, Bruner and Ross (1976). Rudolph Schaffer (2006, 128) defines scaffolding as *the process whereby a more expert partner offers help to a child in problem solving by adjusting both the amount and kind of help to the child's level of performance*. For the child with learning difficulties it is important to ensure that the language used is at an appropriate level for the child's difficulties.

> *Vygotsky was convinced that thinking is not just something that goes on inside an individual's head but it is an activity that can be shared – indeed of necessity has to be shared in the early stages of development. As Rowe and Wertsch (2002) have put it, 'Study of the "I" is thus abandoned in favour of the study of the social, cultural and historically situated ways by which "we" create "I's"'.*

> (Schaffer, 2006)

Critics of scaffolding, for example Stone (1993), argue that the amount of communication that takes place within this interaction is not clearly defined and the effectiveness of the interaction is dependent upon the relationship that exists between adult and child.

This led Barbara Rogoff to define cognitive development as the concept of guided participation. *Cognitive development occurs as new generations collaborate with older generations in varying forms of interpersonal engagement and institutional practices* Rogoff (1998). In this concept the adult acts as a guide to culturally valued practices at a formal level but also allows the child the opportunity to act as observer to informal activities. This puts the child into the role of an 'apprentice'. Rogoff studied a wide range of cultures and concluded that studying the informal joint teaching–learning that takes place in a society allows children to make sense of their society and advance from the present to a more advanced level of understanding.

Learning is then, by these definitions, both an interactive and a social activity. It is this notion that forms the basis of differentiation in teaching. *In planning work for children, a teacher needs to take into account the current state of understanding of the children in question, and plan accordingly and appropriately* (Pritchard, 2005, 31). This has fundamental implications for the way in which we use intervention strategies to help children with learning difficulties. We will return to this later in this chapter when considering teaching and learning strategies.

By contrast, another approach, building on the work of Piaget, is meta-cognitive awareness. This is the understanding an individual has about their own learning processes. Pritchard uses the example of children being told to *Write down these spellings and learn them for a test next week* (2005, 34). The instruction relies upon the child knowing what learning strategies to adopt to successfully complete the task. The child needs to select a method that suits their learning style. This might best be achieved by sharing a range of strategies with the class or group, generating a menu from which the child can, with support, select until the child feels confident to manage this process independently.

Expected development at a given age

In order to fully understand what is meant by the term 'learning difficulties', it is important to recognise what is generally agreed to be the expected development of a child at a given age. For example, when describing the typical achievements of a four-year-old in a Western, English-speaking culture in terms of cognitive development Sharman, et al. (2007, 161–2) identify that the child can:

- build a tower of 10+ bricks and bridges;
- sustain dramatic make-believe play for long periods.

In terms of social development they are:

- capable of sharing and taking turns but may cheat in games in order to win;
- are able to show sympathy for children who are hurt.

Emotionally they are:

- becoming more independent and self-willed, which can lead to conflict;
- are able to show sensitivity to other children and adults.

Children who have not reached this level of achievement at four years old may be described as having learning difficulties. However, it is essential that we consider the whole child in context before we come to any firm conclusions about causal effects. Other factors such as the emotional development of the child, the home environment, fragmentation of the family and social opportunities may also have a bearing on a child's development. In particular, it is important that the child has developed secure and positive attitudes to the adults who are caring for him or her, and has had the opportunity to play with other children. It is also important to recognise that the brain of a young child shows remarkable plasticity, often allowing him or her to recover from the adverse effects of early life experiences and overcome some of the initial learning difficulty.

If you suspect that a child in your class may have learning difficulties you should firstly refer to the expected norms of development for that child's age.

What are learning difficulties?

We need to be clear about what is meant by learning difficulties. The SEN Code of Practice (2001, 86, para 7:58) says that:

Pupils who demonstrate features of moderate, severe or profound learning difficulties or specific learning difficulties, such as dyslexia or dyspraxia, require specific programmes to aid progress in cognition and learning.

This definition is generally accepted to be the one by which schools operate. However, it needs more clarity if it is to be of practical use. The characteristics shown below take us much further towards an accurate judgement.

The characteristics of learning difficulties

Learning difficulties are classified under the following broad headings.

- Moderate learning difficulty (MLD)
- Severe learning difficulty (SLD)
- Profound and multiple learning difficulty (PMLD)
- Specific learning difficulty (SpLD)

These have been defined by the DfES (2005) in the following ways.

Moderate learning difficulty (MLD)
Pupils with moderate learning difficulties will have attainments well below expected levels in all or most areas of the curriculum, despite appropriate interventions. Their needs will not be able to be met by normal differentiation and the flexibilities of the National Curriculum. Pupils with MLD have much greater difficulty than their peers in acquiring basic literacy and numeracy skills and in understanding concepts. They may also have associated speech and language delay, low self-esteem, low levels of concentration and underdeveloped social skills.

Severe learning difficulty (SLD)
Pupils with severe learning difficulties have significant intellectual or cognitive impairments. This has a major effect on their ability to participate in the school curriculum without support.

They may also have associated difficulties in mobility and co-ordination, communication and perception and the acquisition of self-help skills. Pupils with SLD will need support in all areas of the curriculum. They may also require teaching of self-help, independence and social skills. Some pupils may use sign and symbols but most will be able to hold simple conversations and gain some literacy skills. Their attainments may be within the upper P-scale range for much of their school careers (i.e. below level 1 of the National Curriculum).

Profound and multiple learning difficulty (PMLD)

Pupils with profound and multiple learning difficulties have severe and complex learning needs; they also have other significant difficulties such as physical difficulties or a sensory impairment. Pupils require a high level of adult support, both for their learning needs and also for personal care. They are likely to need sensory stimulation and a curriculum broken down into very small steps. Some pupils communicate by gesture, eye pointing or symbols, others by very simple language. Their attainments are likely to remain in the early P-scale range (P1–P4) throughout their school careers (i.e. below level 1 of the National Curriculum).

Specific learning difficulty (SpLD)

'Specific learning difficulties' is an umbrella term, which indicates that pupils display differences across their learning. Pupils with SpLD may have a particular difficulty in learning to read, write, spell or manipulate numbers so that their performance in these areas is below their performance in other areas. Pupils may also have problems with short-term memory, with organisation and with co-ordination. Pupils with SpLD cover the whole ability range and the severity of their impairment varies widely. Specific learning difficulties include dyslexia, dyscalculia and dyspraxia.

Pupils with dyslexia may learn readily in some areas of the curriculum but have a marked and persistent difficulty in acquiring accuracy or fluency in learning to read, write and spell. They may have organisational and memory difficulties.

Pupils with dyscalculia have difficulty in acquiring mathematical skills. Pupils may have difficulty in understanding simple number concepts, lack an intuitive grasp of numbers and have problems learning number facts and procedures.

Pupils with dyspraxia are affected by an impairment or immaturity of the organisation of movement, often appearing clumsy. Gross and fine motor skills are hard to learn and difficult to retain and generalise. Pupils may have poor balance and co-ordination and may be hesitant in many actions (running, skipping, hopping, holding a pencil, doing jigsaws, etc.). Their articulation may also be immature and their language late to develop. They may also have poor awareness of body position. Dyspraxia is often known as developmental co-ordination disorder (DCD).

Pupils with Down's syndrome have a specific chromosomal irregularity that is often associated with learning difficulties. These pupils' needs often span several different areas. They may have speech and language difficulties, sensory impairment, physical and medical needs as well as cognition and learning. Even so, many pupils with Down's syndrome develop well, and learn more than might have been anticipated.

REFLECTIVE TASK

REFLECTIVE TASK

Think back to the children you have encountered on placement.

What examples of struggling learners have you observed?

What were their difficulties?

Do they mirror any of the characteristics shown above?

Teaching and learning strategies

Right up until the late 1990s there was a tendency for special needs teaching to be strongly influenced by behaviourist theories. For example, well-defined objectives were set for teachers and pupils, and systematic methods were available to work towards them (Frederickson and Cline, 2009). These methods were not without their critics (Watson, 2000) argues as follows.

- Teachers became more directive, reduced their expectations of the pupils, set undemanding tasks and neglected to foster meta-cognition, learning strategies and generalisation of learning.
- Pupils became more passive, showed low levels of engagement and low self-esteem, sought a good deal of reassurance and pretended to understand more than they really did.
- Curricula were highly organised and tightly planned, yet lacked intellectual coherence or intrinsic interest.
- Tasks and activities were often solitary with little demand or opportunity for joint or collaborative working.

This led to some children with learning difficulties having tokenistic contact with their peers, mainstream teachers receiving very little training on how to address the needs of these children and little or no classroom support being available to children with special needs in mainstream schools even when they had a statement of educational needs. To illustrate this point read the case studies below.

CASE STUDY
The importance of training

Larry was a Year 6 boy who had severe learning difficulties. He was also dyspraxic and often wore a helmet to avoid an injury when he was playing outside. His parents were keen that he should attend the local primary school that his brother attended. Larry mostly enjoyed the company of his peers although they could find his attentions over-demonstrative at times. This made some children wary of him. The class was made up of 35 children and was mixed Year 5/6. Larry did have a statement of special educational needs and the support of an educational teaching assistant for 15 hours a week, which included any break/lunchtime support. This assistant was very diligent but had received no formal training to support Larry. Today we would say that Larry was operating within the lower end of P scales. He worked best with little distraction and had a designated spot in one corner of the overcrowded room. The teacher designed a curriculum that supported Larry's learning which was mainly carried out by the support assistant. Larry made very little progress in this situation and on transition moved to a special school nearby where he was much happier and made better progress.

CASE STUDY
Finding the best placement

In the late 1980s a teacher in a Year 4 mainstream school in a challenging area was asked to take Susan, a 9-year-old girl with severe learning difficulties who attended a special school, for one afternoon a week. The rationale was that Susan lived in the school's catchment area and would benefit from interaction with her peers in her own neighbourhood. Susan's parents were in favour of this contact. The class teacher was a strong believer in integration and requested a visit to Susan's special school to familiarise herself with Susan's difficulties and to help her plan a series of appropriate activities for the afternoon sessions. Neither the special school nor Susan's school was prepared to offer any classroom support to facilitate this integration. Nevertheless the class teacher was prepared to go ahead and she decided to buddy Susan with two other children in the class. It soon became apparent that Susan found the challenging class stressful. She spoke in very simple sentences and found it difficult to follow the conversations of her peers. Once she lost interest in their conversations she began trying to divert their attention by poking, prodding or hitting them. The teacher had devised a simplified set of tasks which, although appropriate for the girl in her special school where she had almost one-to-one support, were too complex to be tackled without any support in the mainstream classroom. Susan would become distracted by anything around her, including items of simple classroom equipment such as colouring pencils, rulers, scissors or glue, often using them inappropriately. The situation was little better at playtimes when the noise, movement and freedoms of a large area were overwhelming for Susan. The placement lasted for a term but eventually it was agreed that the integration was not successful.

PRACTICAL TASK PRACTICAL TASK **PRACTICAL TASK** PRACTICAL TASK **PRACTICAL TASK**

Discuss the following questions with colleagues.

Were Larry and Susan receiving appropriate teaching and learning?

What were the barriers to their learning?

Was this inclusion?

Fortunately, since those times, cognitive psychology has had an impact on teaching and learning for children with special educational needs. For both children the attempts at inclusion failed. This was possibly because, in both cases, the school was ill-equipped to understand and cater for these individuals' needs. Larry did have some support time but it did not meet his needs in terms of skilled intervention or duration of the support. Susan's special school, her parents and the mainstream class teacher all had her interests at heart, but they were more concerned with her socialisation than her learning. The school did not have the resources to meet her learning needs and was not able to overcome the barriers to her learning. The Code of Practice (DfES, 2001) did improve the quality of provision and the social inclusion for children such as Larry and Susan. It also defined more clearly what it meant by inclusion. The principles of inclusion should include being able to identify learning objectives that set suitable learning challenges, delivered in a way that responded to the learning style of the child and their diverse needs and made accessible to the child in a way that overcame their individual barriers to learning.

REFLECTIVE TASK

REFLECTIVE TASK

Think of an occasion when you have found it difficult to learn a new skill such as learning to drive a car. How did this make you feel? Did the person giving you instruction explain things in simple steps you could follow? Did you compare yourself to others who had already mastered the necessary skills?

It is likely that in such a situation you initially needed to practise certain aspects many times to develop your skills base. You may have needed encouragement to believe in your capacity to complete the task. Your instructor may have scaffolded your learning, gradually withdrawing their support as your confidence and skills developed. You may have felt frustration when your skills did not improve as quickly as you would have liked, or your progress was compared to that of others in the same situation. We now know that a child with cognition and learning needs requires learning objectives in small achievable steps, encouragement to retain focus on tasks and to build self-esteem, and clear instructions repeated as often as necessary.

Learning objectives

Learning objectives need to be closely aligned to the stage of development of the individual and should build on prior achievement in terms of knowledge and understanding. They should be achievable with just the right amount of challenge to allow for success. In practice this will generally involve breaking tasks into very small steps, allowing you to identify any gaps in knowledge and recognise the next step more easily.

Teaching approaches

Your teaching approaches need to provide encouragement to the child and be delivered using a range of learning styles, which are predominantly kinaesthetic and visual in nature. Concrete examples of new concepts are more memorable to all learners. You should give lots of examples and relate the learning to pupils' everyday experiences as frequently as possible. This gives a context to learning. Scaffolding as outlined in the reflective task above is a very powerful strategy. It is important to remember though that support should be gradually withdrawn as a child's understanding and confidence increase. You will need to provide opportunities to practise learning and have infinite patience as you are constantly repeating and reinforcing learning.

Access approaches

There are a number of different access approaches you can use to achieve the above.

- Peer support is a powerful strategy that is often well-received by a child with learning difficulties. It also has a positive effect in terms of inclusion and can free up a teacher's time if used correctly. However, there must always be a sound educational rationale behind its use.
- There are many occasions where introducing new language in the form of key concepts and vocabulary prior to teaching a new concept to the class promotes independence in the learner who may have difficulty grasping new ideas. This is a task that can be undertaken very well by a support assistant and works well as a group activity. You also need to ensure that the meaning of key vocabulary has been clearly understood before learning about the subject can effectively take place.
- Remember to keep your instructions clear and concise. Be prepared to repeat them or to produce them in an alternative format such as pictures.

Helping children to process and record information

Some pupils find it difficult to record their work in written form and you need to consider alternative methods for them. One method is to use visual representations which help pupils to organise their thoughts and communicate meaning. Through this medium we can identify what children already know, and link this to new learning while assessing their understanding. It can also help us to establish how pupils make connections in their ideas which, in turn, can generate talk and support pupils' language development. Similarly, graphic organisers which help pupils to focus upon and understand texts can be useful. They help to develop an awareness of the structure of a text by creating a visual representation and can help to organise information and ideas produced in a formal discussion or written text. In this method each organisational element is represented by a key visual which forms a framework helping the pupil to maintain focus and understanding of the structure of the lesson. It also pinpoints any misconceptions and gives a narrative structure to the development of ideas or learning throughout the lesson. In this way pupils are developing the language associated with classification, making lists, sequencing and prioritising. Mind maps are commonly used in this way as they show how pupils are making connections between ideas and knowledge and how they are grouping these. Another approach that uses the same methodology is the writing frame, which can scaffold pupils' learning by organising their thoughts, allowing them to concentrate upon their ideas in a given way. ICT programs such as Clicker 5 are often used to great effect for this purpose.

Children with learning difficulties often have poor short-term memory. We can help them to store information by using visual aids, modelling the actions we want them to engage in and by repeating instructions ourselves then asking the child to repeat them back to us – rather like the way in which we might repeat a telephone number to commit it to memory.

The Initial Teacher Training Inclusion Development Programme Primary/Secondary: Dyslexia and Speech Language and Communication Needs interactive resource (DCSF, 2008) is a useful guide to specific strategies that are appropriate for children with dyslexia.

Alternatives to written recording

It is often the case that children with learning difficulties find written recording methods overwhelming. Figure 3.1 gives an excellent overview of alternatives to written recording.

The range of strategies includes:

- images;
- charts;
- spoken word;
- ready-made texts;
- ICT;
- sorting and labelling;
- symbols;
- scribing;
- numbers.

Alternatives to written recording

The National Literacy and Numeracy Strategies

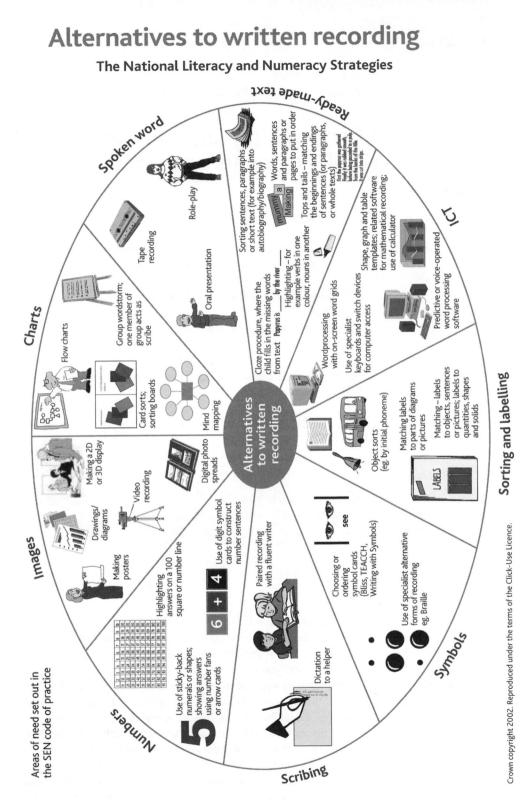

Figure 3.1

Examine each of these strategies in turn. Which have you seen used in your placement schools? Were any not used? Did you see any other strategies used? Which were the most successful?

Suggestions for teaching and learning strategies with key visuals and graphic organisers

- Use graphic devices within text: for example, highlighting, underlining, arrows to connect ideas, bullets and numbers, and space.
- Focus on the language that signals a specific organisational pattern, with opportunities to practise at sentence level where appropriate: for example, using 'so' and 'because' sentences to distinguish between cause and effect.
- Practise sorting, sequencing and ordering anything from objects to information according to different criteria. Encourage pupils to explain their thinking.
- Demonstrate/guided practice of constructing key visuals from text.
- Demonstrate/guided practice of constructing text from key visuals.
- Provide opportunities for pupils to construct visuals that reflect their thinking and understandings.
- This strategy is particularly powerful where pupils have to explain their thinking to others and compare their format with visuals produced from the same text by other pupils.

(Adapted from Special Educational Needs and/or disabilities: A training resource for Initial Teacher Training Providers, 2008)

PRACTICAL TASK PRACTICAL TASK PRACTICAL TASK PRACTICAL TASK PRACTICAL TASK

Read the case study below. Identify the strategies the school used in the teaching and learning of these children. Was the school justified in its use of human resources? Were these children experiencing an inclusive education?

CASE STUDY
A proactive response

A Key Stage 2 class of 28 mixed-aged children had two children with statements of special educational need related to learning difficulties. Additionally, one of the pupils had dyspraxia and medical needs. The second child had dyspraxia and some issues with behaviour. Both children had experienced language and communication difficulties and had been attending speech and language clinics prior to attending school, but on starting school this was withdrawn on the basis that the school had sufficient resources to develop the children's language without further assistance. Each child had some support hours attached to their statement which the school, in consultation with and agreement of the parents, decided to combine, giving almost full-time support coverage in lesson times. The parents of each child supported this approach, acknowledged its value and reasoned that it would help to foster independence while one-to-one support would be more likely to increase dependence on the support assistant. The support provided to each child was identified within their

Individual Education Plan and consisted of a range of strategies appropriate to each child's needs and the task to be undertaken. These included one-to-one with the support assistant to practise skills and develop vocabulary, working as part of their peer group, peer tutoring for basic skills practice, taking part in class lessons both with and without the support assistant. Both children attended a before-school movement programme for children with dyspraxic tendencies run by another support assistant. The class teacher was careful to set the learning objective for each child at the level of the child's ability and understanding and took account of the preferred learning styles of each child. These offered challenge to the individuals in small but realistic steps. Success was celebrated and each child's work was valued, often being placed on display with that of others. One of the children had very low self-esteem in reading and showed no interest in mark-making when they arrived in the class. This child made significant progress and by the end of the year was able to compose a simple sentence. Within the next year the child progressed to writing a paragraph unaided. Both children also took part in school residential visits and the life of the school.

Self-esteem and inclusion for the child with learning difficulties

Both children in the case study made very good progress with their learning. Each success was celebrated and shared with parents as soon as possible. One of the children needed to receive praise very discreetly while the other was happy to be praised in a more public manner. Both children's styles were taken into account. They were fully included in the life of the school and looked forward to coming through the door each day. Their parents felt involved in their child's education and attended review meetings regularly. Visitors to the class rarely noticed the children were receiving addition support. Other children welcomed them as fully participating members of the social group and treated them as equals, often offering discreet support and encouragement if necessary.

It is important to recognise that children with learning difficulties are little different to other children in the class. They do compare themselves to their peers, and the role of the teacher is to facilitate understanding and acceptance of all class members.

A SUMMARY OF **KEY POINTS**

> This chapter has explored what it meant by 'learning' and 'cognition'. It has considered a range of theories about cognition that inform current thinking about how children learn.

> The nature of learning difficulties has been discussed and specific difficulties defined. This led to a discussion about key theoretical approaches and how these could be put into practice for children with learning difficulties, and then offered a range of teaching strategies to support teaching and learning.

> The case studies gave an insight into past and current practice which exemplified the advances in our understanding that have taken place in the last few years. They show a marked improvement in the inclusive practices that exist today.

> In the words of *Every Child Matters* (2003), our aim must be to facilitate enjoyment and achievements of children with learning difficulties to get the most out of life and develop broad skills for adulthood.

MOVING *ON* > > > > > > MOVING *ON* > > > > > > MOVING *ON*

When you are next on placement, make a study of a child who has learning difficulties in the class who has an Individual Education Plan (IEP). Find out what strategies have been identified on this IEP. In consultation with the class teacher consider if these are working successfully and discuss the next steps the school intends to take.

REFERENCES REFERENCES **REFERENCES** REFERENCES **REFERENCES** REFERENCES

Claxton, G. (2008) *What is the point of school?* Oxford: Oneworld.

Department for Education and Skills (2001) Special Educational Needs Code of Practice, Ref. DfES/ 581/2001. London: DfES.

Department for Education and Skills (2003) *Every Child Matters*. Norwich: TSO.

Department for Education and Skills (2005) Data Collection by Type of Special Educational Need. Ref. DfES/1889/2005. Nottingham: DfES Publications.

Frederickson, N. and Cline, T. (2009) *Special Educational Needs, Inclusion and Diversity*, 2nd edition. Maidenhead: Open University Press.

Gardner, H. (1983) *Frames of Mind*. London: Heinemann.

Garner, P. (2009) *Special Educational Needs: The Key Concepts*. Abingdon: Routledge.

Jarvis, M. (2005) *The psychology of effective teaching and learning*. Cheltenham: Nelson Thornes.

Penn, H. (2008) *Understanding Early Childhood Issues and Controversies*, 2nd edition. Maidenhead: Open University Press.

Pritchard, A. (2005) *Ways of Learning. Learning Theories and Learning Styles in the Classroom*. Abingdon: Fulton.

Rogoff, B. (1998) 'Cognition as a collaborative process', in W. Damon (ed) *Handbook of child psychology*, vol. 2 (D. Kuhn and R.S. Siegler, eds). New York: Wiley.

Rudolph Schaffer, H. (2006) *Key Concepts in Developmental Psychology*. London: Sage.

Sharman, C., Cross, W. and Vennis, D. (2007) *Observing Children and Young People*, 4th edition. London: Continuum.

Tassoni, P. (2003) *Supporting Special Needs Understanding Inclusion in the Early Years*. Oxford: Heinemann

TDA (2008) *Special Educational Needs and/ or disabilities: A training resource for initial teacher training providers: primary undergraduate courses*. London: TDA.

Vygotsky, L. (1978) *Mind in Society*. Cambridge, MA: Harvard University Press.

Watson, J. (2000) 'Constructive instruction and learning difficulties', *Support for Learning*, 15 (3), 134–140.

Wood, D. (1998) *How Children Think and Learn*, 2nd edition. Oxford: Blackwell.

Wood, D., Bruner, J. and Ross, G. (1976) 'The role of tutoring in problem solving', *Journal of Child Psychology and Child Psychiatry*, 17, 89–100.

FURTHER READING FURTHER READING **FURTHER READING** FURTHER READING

Department for Children, Schools and Families (2008) Initial Teacher Training Inclusion Development Programme Primary/Secondary: Dyslexia and Speech Language and Communication Needs, Ref. 00103-2008DVD-EN

McGee, P. (2001) *Thinking Psychologically*. Basingstoke: Palgrave.

Stoll, L., Fink, D. and Earl, L. (2003) *It's About Learning (and About Time). What's in it for schools?* London: RoutledgeFalmer.

Useful website

www.nationalstrategies.standards.dcsf.gov.uk/inclusion/specialeducationalneeds

PART 2
TEACHING SPECIAL
EDUCATIONAL NEEDS

4
Supporting children with reading difficulties

Chapter objectives

By the end of this chapter you should be aware of:

- **theories that help to explain the causes of dyslexia;**
- **the impact of dyslexia on pupils' self-esteem;**
- **strategies to support children with reading difficulties.**

This chapter addresses the following Professional Standards for the award of QTS:

Q1, Q2, Q6, Q14, Q19

Introduction

This chapter focuses on dyslexia and provides examples of strategies for supporting children who fall within this group. However, we wish to emphasise that in focusing on learners with dyslexia, we do not wish to exclude those children who may have reading difficulties but have not been diagnosed as dyslexic. Many children with general reading difficulties will have similar problems to those who are dyslexic. The distinction between those who are dyslexic and those with reading difficulties will be explored further in this chapter. Within the chapter we draw upon the social model of disability and we emphasise that with appropriate teaching interventions and positive attitudes, teachers can and do make a difference to children who find reading difficult. We examine the impact of dyslexia on children's self-esteem and we discuss strategies for developing a dyslexia-friendly learning environment.

What is dyslexia?

'Dyslexia' is by no means a new word. In 1878 Kussmaul wrote about 'text blindness': He stated that:

> A complete text-blindness may exist even though the power of sight, the intellect, and the power of speech are intact.
>
> (Kussmaul, 1878, in Miles and Miles, 1990, 3)

Shortly after the writings of Kussmaul, the concept of 'word-blindness' was used to explain difficulties in learning to read in apparently intelligent children. Word-blindness was given prominence in medical literature for the next two decades. The writings of a Glasgow eye surgeon, James Hinshelwood in 1917, made links between congenital word-blindness and reading failure. Hinshelwood (1917, cited in Miles and Miles, 1990, 5) also noted that the condition might be hereditary and was more common in boys than in girls.

The American neurologist Samuel Orton, writing in 1937, was critical of the term 'congenital word-blindness', arguing that it was misleading:

> *There is no true blindness in the ordinary sense of the term nor, indeed, is there even blindness for words.*
>
> (Orton, 1937, cited in Miles and Miles, 1990, 5)

Orton noticed a tendency for these types of children to distort the order of the letters in words in spoken and written language. Orton introduced the term 'strephosymbolia', which literally means 'twisting of symbols' to describe this syndrome. Orton, along with Anna Gillingham, pioneered a systematic teaching programme, aimed specifically at pupils who had these problems.

Both Hinshelwood and Orton are respected as great pioneers in this field. Causation for reading difficulties was linked to visual problems and diagnosis of dyslexia centred on looking for an overuse of 'reversals' of letters or 'mirror writing'. Later research cast doubt on the value of this visual model and towards the end of the twentieth century, the emphasis shifted to a phonological model as an explanation for children with dyslexia. The work of Hinshelwood and Orton in the early twentieth century and their observations are, according to Miles and Miles (1999), *of lasting importance*.

The actual word 'dyslexia' is made from a combination of two Greek words: *Dys,* which literally means 'difficult', 'painful' or 'abnormal', and *lexicos*, which means 'words of a language'. Hence, a literal translation is 'difficulty with words'. According to Riddick *at a common-sense everyday level, dyslexia is often defined as an unexpected difficulty in learning to read, write or spell* (Riddick, 1996, 1).

The media perpetuate the image of the tragedy of the intelligent child who has failed to learn to read. In this sense, dyslexia is commonly defined as a discrepancy between a child's level of intelligence and their reading skills. The difficulty is therefore unexpected and specific and prevents the child from achieving their great potential. Some working definitions have high-lighted this discrepancy, for example:

> *Dyslexia is a disorder manifested by a difficulty in learning to read despite conventional instruction, adequate intelligence and sociocultural opportunity. It is dependent upon fundamental cognitive disabilities, which are frequently of constitutional origin.*
>
> (World Federation of Neurology, 1968, cited in Riddick, 1996, 2)

Lowenstein (1989) favours a definition of dyslexia which highlights the discrepancy between verbal intelligence and reading ability. Such definitions fail to include children who have difficulties learning to read but also have below-average levels of IQ. The term *garden variety poor readers* (Stanovich, 1988, 96) has been used to categorise children with low levels of IQ and poor reading skills. Poor readers are therefore differentiated as either 'discrepant' or 'non-discrepant' readers. Within these definitions, IQ is taken as an accepted measure of intelligence. The notion of IQ as a reliable measure of intelligence has been contested. In addition, the use of IQ fails to take into account the notion of multiple intelligence (Gardner). There are many famous people with dyslexia who have become skilled artists, sports people or musicians. Therefore it seems unethical to exclude such talented individuals from a diagnosis of dyslexia simply on the grounds that they may have below-average levels of IQ.

Arguments against such definitions are further strengthened by research which has investigated the reading profiles of learners with and without dyslexia, classified as such under the discrepancy model (Stanovich and Stanovich, 1997). This research has found that the reading profiles of both groups do not differ. It is therefore logical to conclude that IQ is irrelevant and should not be taken into account when defining or diagnosing dyslexia. Some definitions are more inclusive and do not refer to intelligence. For example:

> *Dyslexia is evident when accurate and fluent word reading and/or spelling develops very incompletely or with great difficulty... it provides the basis for a staged process of assessment through teaching.*
>
> (British Psychological Society, 1999, 11)

> *Dyslexia is a specific learning difficulty that hinders the learning of literacy skills... and tends to run in families. Other symbolic systems, such as mathematics and musical notation, can also be affected. Dyslexia can occur at any level of intellectual ability. It can accompany, but is not a result of, lack of motivation, emotional disturbance, sensory impairment or meagre opportunities...*
>
> (The Dyslexia Institute, 1996, cited in Turner, 1997, 11)

These definitions do not make a distinction between dyslexic readers and poor readers with low intelligence. However, the second definition is broader than the first. The BPS definition focuses on literacy difficulties at word level but the second definition by the Dyslexia Institute focuses on difficulties with symbolic systems in general. In 1989 the International Dyslexia Association adopted a broad definition to include aspects of literacy, numeracy, difficulties with information processing, motor skills and behaviour. In view of these debates it is not difficult to see why dyslexia has become a *professional battlefield* (Swan, 1985, cited in Riddick, 1996, 21).

Types of dyslexia

The key sub-types of dyslexia are identified below.

Phonological dyslexia

Phonological dyslexics have specific difficulties remembering letter names and sounds and they find it difficult to make sound–symbol relationships. They find it difficult to blend sounds together to read words, they struggle to read non-words and they may find it difficult to detect rhyme.

Surface or morphemic dyslexia

These children appear to master the alphabetic code but over-rely on a phonological strategy for reading and spelling. Irregular words are often pronounced as though they are regular, for example, the word 'island' may be pronounced as 'izland' (Snowling, 1998). These learners generally have no difficulty reading non-words but they may struggle to read sight words, due to an over-reliance on the use of phonology.

Hyperlexia

Hyperlexics have good visual memories and are able to learn sight words. They are able to learn sound–symbol relationships and can therefore blend sounds together to read words. The main problem lies in understanding or remembering what they have read. They often struggle to create meaning in their written work, although spelling may be accurate (Hall, 2009).

Causes of dyslexia

Visual deficit theories

Research by Stein and Walsh (1997) indicated evidence of a magnocellular deficit. The magnocells are the nerve cells in the eyes and they are linked to the visual area of the brain. Defects in the magnocells disrupt the transfer of visual information between the eyes and the brain. An impaired visual system can result in reduced focus, blurred vision, headaches and the formation of unstable images (Hall, 2009). Acknowledgement of dyslexia as a visual deficit often results in a variety of intervention strategies that aim to reduce the glare from white paper. Such strategies include the use of coloured overlays, coloured paper or tinted lenses.

Phonological deficit hypothesis

Since the 1980s several studies have highlighted phonological processing difficulties in children with dyslexia (Shankweiler and Crain, 1986; Share, 1995; Snowling, 1995, all cited in Snowling, 1998). Snowling (1998) argues that children with dyslexia find it difficult to retrieve phonological information from the long-term memory. Dyslexia is now accepted as a developmental language disorder rather than a visual deficit disorder.

You need to understand theoretical perspectives of how children learn to read before you can develop a full understanding of the phonological deficit model. Bradley and Bryant's research in 1983 showed the relationship between early phonological awareness and subsequent reading acquisition. Thus, children with good early phonological awareness (sound discrimination, understanding of rhyme) are more likely to be good readers in primary school. Sound discrimination and an understanding of rhyme are essential pre-reading skills. If children fail to pick up similarities and differences between sounds they hear and words that are spoken to them, it is possible that they will find it more difficult to discriminate between sounds in words when they start to learn to read.

Uta Frith (1985) provides a theoretical model of the stages children go through when they learn to read. These stages can be summarised as follows.

Logographic stage

Children remember words as if they are a logo or a picture. Very young children can recognise environmental print but they are not able to draw on strategies to decipher unfamiliar words. At this stage children memorise word shapes and colours. Think about how children learn to 'read' shop signs, for example. At this stage children rely on a visual strategy for reading words.

Alphabetic stage

At this stage children begin to link letters and sounds together (i.e. they make grapheme–phoneme correspondences). Spelling at this stage tends to reflect an increasing awareness of sounds and may be largely phonetic. At this stage children will start to sound out unfamiliar words through blending the sounds together.

Orthographic stage

At this stage the child is able to memorise spelling patterns, as well as being able to recognise common prefixes and suffixes. They are able to segment words into syllables and they are able to read by analogy. For example, they are able to read the word 'fright' because they recognise the word 'light'.

Frith (1985) suggests that in the case of learners with dyslexia, development becomes arrested at the logographic stage. They fail to make quick and automatic links between letters and their sounds. They may find it difficult to 'sound out' words and they depend on a small sight vocabulary.

According to Snowling (1998, 6), *they continue to rely for longer than normal readers on a visual strategy for reading words and many have persisting difficulties reading novel words that are not part of their sight vocabulary, such as non-words*.

Therefore it is important to understand why phonological dyslexics may struggle to master the alphabetic code or experience difficulties with early phonological awareness. Abnormalities in the language area of the brain may interfere with the learning of symbol–sound relationships (Hall, 2009). In addition, slow processing speeds in general and poor short-term memory may impede the ability to make quick and automatic links between letters and sounds. You could find that learners with dyslexia need to be exposed longer to letters, colours, shapes, numbers or words in order to memorise them. Therefore the phonological deficit which occurs as a result of abnormalities in the brain is made worse as a result of slow processing speeds, and this has been referred to as a 'double-deficit hypothesis'. Research has also indicated that morphemic dyslexics do not perform at age-related norms on phonological tasks, despite the fact that eventually they start to over-rely heavily on a phonological strategy (Manis *et al.*, 1996; Stanovich *et al.*, 1997). According to Snowling (1998, 7), it would appear *that the severity of a child's phonological difficulty can affect the way in which their reading system becomes set up – and whether they look like 'phonological' or 'surface' dyslexics*. Dyslexia has therefore been defined as a core phonological deficit (Stanovich, 1986) and this implies that the intervention strategies should operate at a phonological level rather than a visual level.

Genetic factors

There is now a clear research base to suggest that genetic factors can increase the likelihood of dyslexia (Taipale *et al.*, 2003 ; Schumacher *et al.*, 2007, cited in Hall, 2009). A boy with one dyslexic parent has a 50 per cent chance of being dyslexic and the chances are increased if the parent is the father (Hall, 2009). However, caution needs to be exercised about these arguments. It is not inevitable that the 'genetic gene' will be passed onto the child (Hall, 2009, 12) and the brain *develops as a result of the interplay between environmental factors, stimulation of the brain as well as genetic factors* (Hall, 2009, 12). The problem with biological arguments is that they perpetuate the idea that dyslexia is a personal tragedy caused by 'within-child' factors and that little can be done about it. The social model, in contrast, acknowledges the impairment but urges practitioners to make modifications to their teaching style so that the impairment does not become a disability. Thus, with changes to teaching style and the use of access strategies, pupils with dyslexia can, and do, learn to read very successfully.

Defining characteristics

As a classroom teacher you will not be responsible for carrying out psychometric tests on children in order to diagnose dyslexia. Qualified psychologists will be responsible for such assessments. However, it is useful to be able to identify any warning signs through regular ongoing formative assessment. The following prompts may help you.

- Does the child have persistent difficulties with reading?
- Does the child find it difficult to learn grapheme–phoneme correspondences?
- Is the child reluctant to read or write?
- Does the child have persistent spelling difficulties? Spelling may be bizarre.
- Does the child have problems with personal organisation or display sequencing difficulties (e.g. learning the order of days of the week)?
- Does the child find it difficult to tell the time?
- Does the child have a poor short-term memory (e.g. remembering instructions or forgetting to bring things to school on certain days)?
- Does the child find rote learning difficult (e.g. memorising multiplication tables)?
- Does the child demonstrate inappropriate behaviour to avoid certain situations?
- Does the child have poor concentration or find it difficult to process information?
- Does the child have poor motor skills or difficulties with co-ordination?

Clearly these points cannot be used to diagnose dyslexia. They simply provide a loose framework for identifying whether a referral for more specialised support is necessary. Hall (2009) provides a very comprehensive checklist for warning signs to look out for in the Early Years, at Key Stage 1 and at Key Stage 2. Early Years educators should pay careful attention to young children who find rhyming difficult (Hall, 2009). In addition, children with dyslexia may have speech problems or difficulties with motor skills such as climbing stairs or riding a bike (Hall, 2009). They may be slow to write their own name and may find it difficult to make grapheme–phoneme correspondences (Hall, 2009). At Key Stage 1 children may find blending difficult or they may find it difficult to learn sight words and they may struggle with writing (Hall, 2009). Although learners with dyslexia may overcome their reading difficulties, it is possible that they will experience persistent difficulties with spelling, and Hall (2009) identifies that spelling may become increasingly random and idiosyncratic at Key Stage 2.

As a teacher it is important that you listen to parental concerns and take them seriously. Riddick (1995, 462) found that there was an average time of four years elapsing between the parents first suspecting that there was a problem and their children receiving an official diagnosis of dyslexia. Some of the parents in this study expressed their concerns:

> *I thought something was up. I was told I was an overprotective mother and Dean was just a slow learner and there was nothing wrong. And I probably being foolish*

left it and the next year we went to parents evening and there was absolutely no progress and again I voiced my opinion and again I was told I was being silly.

(Riddick, 1995, 465)

The thing the teacher did say once, that irritates me now, was that she was very slow at school, slow to learn. And basically, she's not slow to learn. It was the reading that she was slow to learn. And I think that was a lack of understanding.

(Riddick, 1996, 88)

A reluctance to take parental concerns seriously can slow down the process of diagnosis and result in parents becoming frustrated.

Diagnosing dyslexia

As a general classroom teacher you are not qualified to make a diagnosis of dyslexia. If you have ongoing concerns that a child may be dyslexic you are likely to have placed the child on School Action Plus in consultation with the SENCO and parent(s). You will therefore be able to bring in external support to help you meet the needs of the child. For example, an educational psychologist will be able to suggest particular teaching approaches to enable the child to make further progress. In addition, s/he will also be able to carry out more detailed assessments which may indicate the likelihood of a child having dyslexia. These additional assessments can supplement your own teacher assessments and both can then be used as evidence to support an application for a statutory assessment by the local authority.

Some parents may choose to have their child assessed by a dyslexia-trained teacher in a specialist centre. These teachers have carried out additional training and are qualified to make a specific diagnosis. As a classroom teacher you may wish to ask the SENCO to purchase specialist screening software and tests which you will be able to use. These will not make a diagnosis of dyslexia as such, but may provide an indicator of the likely chance of a child being dyslexic. It is important that teachers do not provide a specific diagnosis when these assessments are shared with parent(s).

Labelling

One of the key dangers associated with the use of labels is that it can result in a 'within-child' view of the problem. The whole process of observation, assessment, diagnosis and intervention seems to resemble the medical model of disability where disability is conceptualised as a personal tragedy. Labels and categories can also impose on individuals a 'fixed' identity. In essence, people within the specific category are all associated as having similar needs and it may be assumed that they will be equally responsive to interventions.

As a teacher you must remember that children with dyslexia are individuals. Although they may share some defining characteristics, they will not respond in the same way to interventions and they will have different needs. You have a responsibility to the child to develop teaching approaches that are specific to that child. Reading recovery may not work for all learners with dyslexia in the same way that a visual timetable may not work for all learners with autistic spectrum disorder. Rather than adopting a medical model approach, you should aim to adopt a social model approach. This focuses on placing less emphasis on intervening at the level of the individual and placing more emphasis on ways in which you can develop more effective teaching strategies that will benefit not just learners with dyslexia, but all learners. Think carefully about wider aspects of your practice, which may result in barriers to achievement. For example, do you use too much text in lessons? Do you ask children to read aloud? Do you overemphasise auditory rather than visual and kinaesthetic teaching approaches? Do you ask children to record their work in a range of ways, or do you ask them to record through writing? Your practice can erect barriers to achievement for many learners and this should be your starting point. Focus on how you can make adaptations to your practice before you place too much emphasis on 'within-child' factors.

Riddick (1995) found that the official diagnosis of dyslexia was an important milestone for children: the use of the terminology helped them to understand their problems and helped to raise their self-esteem. The term helped them to understand why they had difficulties and they found it empowering (Riddick, 1995). Riddick also found that the parents were pleased with the official diagnosis and they were able to use it to prove to the teachers that there was a genuine problem. One parent in Riddick's study commented:

> Well I was thrilled. I've got the assessment he had here . . . I took it to school, you know. Vindicated! Rubbish, they said. There's no such thing as dyslexia.
>
> (Riddick, 1995, 462)

One key problem with the use of the term 'dyslexia' is that it distinguishes between learners with dyslexia and those children with general reading difficulties. It could therefore be argued that the term excludes a group of poor readers who need support and intervention. The strategies suggested in this chapter will help all children with reading difficulties and as a teacher you will need to implement interventions with all learners working below age-related expectations in reading. However, although we have highlighted the exclusive nature of the term, we assert that dismissive attitudes towards dyslexia are extremely unhelpful. Thus, teachers need to reflect carefully on their own attitudes towards children with special educational needs since they are unlikely to undertake further professional development and training if they do not believe that a condition exists.

CASE STUDY
Issues with labelling

Jasmine was ten years old. She had recently been given a diagnosis of dyslexia after struggling for many years with reading and writing. She was able to sound out simple consonant-vowel-consonant (CVC) words but she could not remember the phonemes for more complex graphemes, such as digraphs. Jasmine's mother was thrilled with the diagnosis and had tried to use this to pressurise the school to provide Jasmine with additional support. Jasmine did not respond positively to reading or writing tasks. On several occasions she was overhead to say *I can't read or write because I am dyslexic.* The teacher had worked hard to develop Jasmine's self-esteem. She had provided Jasmine with one-to-one support and Jasmine had had access to a rich multi-sensory phonics programme. Despite this, progress in reading and writing was minimal.

- What was the impact of the diagnosis on Jasmine?
- What was the impact of the diagnosis on Jasmine's mother?
- What might the teacher do next to support Jasmine?

Impact of dyslexia on self-esteem

According to Lawrence (1996, xi), *one of the most exciting discoveries in educational psychology in recent times has been the finding that people's levels of achievement are influenced by how they feel about themselves (and vice-versa)*. Although this seems obvious, it is a point worth making. As a teacher, a major part of your role is to nurture within children a positive sense of self. If children feel good about themselves this will create optimum conditions for effective learning.

Research has indicated that children with learning difficulties make negative and unrealistic comparisons between themselves and others and, as a result of this, develop low levels of self-esteem (Gurney, 1988; Humphrey, 2001, 2003). Consequently they may feel inferior to their peers and this can have far-reaching consequences. Although there is a lack of research on the links between dyslexia and self-esteem (Humphrey, 2002), some studies have high-lighted feelings of disappointment, frustration, anger and embarrassment (Edwards, 1994; Riddick, 1996). Studies have also revealed how some dyslexics feel that were treated unfairly by teachers (Riddick, 1996; Humphrey, 2001; Humphrey and Mullins, 2002) and also their peers (Humphrey, 2001).

My own unpublished research (Glazzard, 2004) produced findings which were consistent with the findings in the published studies cited above. Some of the children's voices are shown below and highlight the negative attitudes demonstrated by some teachers and peers towards children with reading difficulties.

Attitude of teachers

The study highlighted both negative and positive attitudes from teachers:

I had one teacher who I had for a year [Mrs X]. My friend had her as well. She was really against kids who had learning difficulties. She didn't like Asian kids either and she didn't like boys. She was really, really mean to us. Like me and J were really good friends and she was really nasty to us ... She used to call us stupid and that we'd fail at this and that. Anything she could to be nasty she'd say it for no reason at all. (David)

The headmaster was absolutely brilliant ... Mr F. I'd go and read to him and when he was teaching us I'd say can you just say that again and he'd repeat it ... Mrs. D (special needs support assistant) helped me a lot. (Chris)

I can't remember any by name but there were some in ... the infants that weren't supportive ... They were getting onto me about why I wasn't doing as much and they moaned when I always came bottom in the spelling test. (James)

In primary school they used to make us read aloud and I always dreaded it 'cos I knew the others would laugh at me. I knew that they were better readers than I was. I can't really blame them for laughing 'cos they didn't know I had dyslexia at that point and neither did I. (Sam)

Well, none of them really understood it. They just left it to this one teacher. She was the special needs teacher... She was basically the only teacher that helped. The others just let me get on with it. (Nick)

(Glazzard, 2004)

REFLECTIVE TASK
REFLECTIVE TASK

Think carefully about the attitudes above. Discuss the following questions with one of your colleagues.

How might you adapt a spelling test for a child with dyslexia?

How might you present reading material to children with dyslexia to make it more inclusive?

How do you think Mrs X might change her practice to make it more inclusive?

Why might 'reading aloud' be an unsuitable strategy for children with dyslexia?

Feeling stupid

My reading was worse than the other kids. I couldn't read anything. I had to sound everything out. So 'dog' was 'd-o-g'. It really slowed me down and made me feel stupid. I also struggled with maths. (Tom)

(Glazzard, 2004)

REFLECTIVE TASK
REFLECTIVE TASK

What strategies might help Tom to develop a more positive sense of self? Think carefully about how you might build in frequent opportunities for Tom to experience success. Share your ideas with a colleague.

Attitude of peers

My friends have always supported me. They've always been good friends. As for other people, I keep it to myself. I don't let them know. It's my life, not theirs. Some of them know and they're always grinning and laughing because I work more slowly in class and find spelling difficult. They have made nasty comments to me. But they don't know what it's like 'cos they're not dyslexic. (Paul)

(Glazzard, 2004)

REFLECTIVE TASK
REFLECTIVE TASK

What strategies might you use to address the issues that Paul highlights?

Comparisons with peers

I knew I wasn't as good at spelling as the other pupils were because I never got many correct. (Stuart)

Do you think it is more important to work on developing Stuart's self-esteem or on developing his reading skills? Where would you place the emphasis? How can you develop more inclusive practices so that children are less likely to make comparisons between themselves and their peers?

Riddick (1996) has highlighted the reluctance of some teachers to accept the fact that a child may have dyslexia. This can result in feelings of frustration from parents who may be desperately trying to obtain educational support for their child. *Removing barriers to achievement* (DfES, 2004) stresses the need for early intervention to enable children to make further progress. If teachers fail to take parental concerns seriously and adopt a dismissive attitude towards dyslexia, then intervention will be delayed.

PRACTICAL TASK PRACTICAL TASK PRACTICAL TASK PRACTICAL TASK PRACTICAL TASK

Nosheen is six years old. She finds reading difficult and she is making very slow progress. Her mother approaches you and expresses a concern that she may be dyslexic because of the lack of interest she shows in books. Nosheen's mother is also concerned that other children have made greater progress and are reading more difficult reading books. Discuss the following questions with a colleague.

What do you think you might say to Nosheen's mother? What advice might you offer her?

What subsequent action might you take to show the mother that you have taken her concerns seriously?

My own unpublished research (Glazzard, 2004) illustrates the impact of a diagnosis of dyslexia on pupils' sense of self:

> *At last I realised I wasn't stupid. I had a problem but it wasn't related to my intelligence. (Chris)*

The diagnosis therefore came as a relief to pupils and this is consistent with findings in published research (Riddick, 1996). Parents may also value an official diagnosis of dyslexia, believing that it will inevitably lead to additional funding and support. Therefore there may be value in obtaining a diagnosis. However, the extent of the child's needs ultimately determines whether additional provision will be made available. You should not assume that a diagnosis of dyslexia will automatically result in additional funding and support.

PRACTICAL TASK PRACTICAL TASK PRACTICAL TASK PRACTICAL TASK PRACTICAL TASK

Can you think about ways in which labelling children in this way may be detrimental to children? Discuss this with a colleague and then look for literature which explores arguments for and against labelling. Share these ideas with your group in the form of a ten-minute presentation.

Strategies to support children with reading difficulties

The following strategies should help you to meet the needs of learners with dyslexia. However, it is important to stress that you need to respond to the specific needs of individual learners.

Multi-sensory teaching

Multi-sensory approaches are generally inclusive and work for all children. When you are introducing children to graphemes and phonemes, all the senses need to be stimulated. They need to see the letter, feel the shape of the letter and they should be encouraged to say the phoneme at the same time. Children should be encouraged to 'air write' the letter or to write it on someone else's back or the palm of the hand. They should be encouraged to make the letter shapes out of dough and draw them in the sand or trace it in the water. Sandpaper letters are useful for learners with dyslexia to feel the shape of letters. In PE children can be encouraged to make letter shapes with their bodies. These are practical suggestions for ways in which you can build visual, auditory and kinaesthetic approaches into your teaching.

A structured programme

Learners with dyslexia will need a highly structured phonics programme. Reading recovery is one example of such a programme and is described below. Lessons may have a similar structure but the content of each will vary to ensure progression and continuity.

Over-learning

Children with dyslexia often have problems with short-term memory. They may quickly forget graphemes, phonemes and words that they have been taught. You will need to build in opportunities for revisiting learning that has taken place.

Reading recovery

Reading recovery started several years ago but is now the approach used within the government's Every Child a Reader (ECAR) programme. The programme is individualised for each child and constitutes a Wave 3 intervention programme.

Teaching spelling and handwriting

Broomfield and Combley (2003) recommend a cursive script where all letters start with a stroke from the base line and end with a leaving stroke. This approach means that the learner does not have to think about where the letter begins as all letters start in the same place. Learners with dyslexia need to practise writing the letter at the same time as being introduced to the phoneme. This is because the action of actually forming the letter and saying the phoneme at the same time will deepen the learning experience. The sound should always be linked to a hand movement. You will need to make decisions about whether to introduce your learners to a joined script. Broomfield and Combley (2003) stress the importance of movement when introducing children to letters. They emphasise that *the learner needs to be aware of the air moving from the lungs, and being shaped by tongue, lips and throat* (Broomfield and Combley, 2003, 106).

Waves of intervention

The National Strategies promote a three-staged model to raise outcomes for all children. This is summarised below.

Wave 1: Inclusive quality first teaching for all children.
Wave 2: Additional interventions (usually group interventions) to enable children to meet age-related expectations.
Wave 3: Highly personalised interventions to meet the specific needs of individual learners.

(TDA, 2008)

Before a child is diagnosed as dyslexic it is therefore important to establish whether that child has been exposed to inclusive quality first teaching. Quality first teaching of reading has been described in the Independent Review of the Teaching of Early Reading (DfES, 2006) as teaching which uses a multi-sensory approach and is informed by assessment to meet the needs of individual learners. The report recommended that phonic skills should be taught discreetly and within the context of a broad and rich language curriculum. Therefore it is important to question whether struggling readers have had access to rich multi-sensory teaching programmes which meet their specific needs before it is assumed that they may have a reading difficulty. It is also important to examine whether they have had access to a rich literate environment both at home and in school. This includes ensuring that children can access texts that interest them. Parents and teachers act as role models for reading and writing. If children see parents and teachers enjoying reading and writing, there is a greater chance that they too will be motivated. If children with literacy difficulties have not had exposure to role models, then this could, in part, explain an apparent lack of motivation to read or write. Some schools enlist the support of famous football players or fathers by asking them to work alongside children in the classroom as readers or writers. This could be a particularly powerful way of raising boys' achievements in literacy, given that dyslexia is more common among boys. As a teacher you also need to think carefully about the inter-relationship between the different strands of literacy and the powerful role of speaking and listening in raising standards in reading and writing. Your literate environment should provide opportunities for frequent talk, drama or role-play. Children may develop reading difficulties as a result of poor-quality teaching and exposure to poor learning environments. Although biological factors may also be significant, teachers should not underestimate the importance of quality first teaching.

If, despite exposure to quality first teaching, children develop reading difficulties, teachers should provide small-group (Wave 2) or individual (Wave 3) interventions to meet the specific needs of individual learners. Reading recovery has been described above and constitutes a Wave 3 intervention programme. *Removing barriers to achievement* (DfES, 2004) stresses the importance of early intervention and support and teachers should take early action to give children every opportunity to catch up with their peers.

Dyslexia-friendly environments

Pupils with dyslexia typically find reading and writing difficult. You need therefore to provide these pupils with alternative ways of recording information. Pupils can document their learning visually, orally and practically, as well as using ICT. You might find that a pupil with dyslexia has a talent in science. However, if you ask them to write up an investigation this might demotivate them. Try to be creative in your approaches. Teachers typically like to collect recorded work for assessment evidence. However, you can broaden your range of evidence through documenting the learning that has taken place through the use of teacher observations, photographs, and video recordings of pupils at work, as well as audio-recordings of children's conversations. This is common practice in the Early Years and should be built on in Key Stages 1 and 2.

Try not to ask children with dyslexia to copy from the board or to read out in class. You need to be both sympathetic and empathetic. Children with dyslexia need to know that you understand their difficulties. Some children will find it easier if material is presented on cream or buff paper, as white paper can make words difficult to read. Children with dyslexia need constructive feedback on their work. An overemphasis on spelling errors is unhelpful and you should focus on the content of the work instead. Children with dyslexia will need lots of positive reinforcement when they read to you.

Children with dyslexia may have good ideas but may struggle to write these ideas down on paper. They may benefit from a scribe or a study buddy, who can help them record their ideas. Short-term memory may be a problem so teach children strategies to help them remember things. They will need to be taught spelling and reading strategies explicitly and a structured programme to support reading and spelling is essential. You could try pairing children with dyslexia with an older reader who can read to them or support them with reading. Children with dyslexia need to read books which are interesting and you should avoid giving them books which are suitable for younger readers as this could damage self-esteem.

Mathematical learning may be difficult for children with dyslexia as they may quickly forget things. Ensure that there is access to number lines, number squares and practical apparatus to support learning. Try to ensure that your learners understand the learning rather than focusing excessively on how many calculations or problems they have solved within a lesson. They may need access to a calculator to help with problem-solving, even if other learners are required to complete a task mentally. In particular, learners with dyslexia may struggle with multiplication tables so you will need to find creative, innovative ways of teaching these.

The classroom should have key words on display for learners to refer to. You could also give these learners additional resources such as word mats, alphabet strips or special dictionaries to support them with spelling. Portable writing aids such as word processors, tablets, hand-held spell checkers or palmtop devices can be useful. Concept mapping tools on the computer can be useful to enable learners with dyslexia to plan and organise information.

PRACTICAL TASK PRACTICAL TASK **PRACTICAL TASK** PRACTICAL TASK **PRACTICAL TASK**

In your placement school identify a child with dyslexia. Discuss the specific needs of the child with your teacher-mentor. Find out about prior learning and plan for the child's 'next steps'. Over the period of a week, plan a series of multi-sensory activities to enable the child to make further progress. Evaluate each taught session and make regular assessments of the child's learning. Evaluate the overall progress of the child and write a synoptic critical reflection summarising your own learning from this experience.

CASE STUDY
Multi-sensory intervention

Joshua was six years old. After more than a year in school it was evident that Joshua had some difficulties with the acquisition of phonic knowledge. He could not remember many phonemes and he could not blend sounds together to read words. His teacher decided to provide some additional intervention to enable Joshua to make further progress. A multi-sensory programme was developed to help Joshua to learn the simple alphabetic code. Further progress in reading would be hampered unless Joshua could master the simple alphabetic code. Each lesson was clearly structured, starting with a recap on phonemes which had previously been taught. Any misconceptions at this point became the focus of the lesson. Phonemes were taught in a multi-sensory way. The letter was shown to Joshua and he was told the phoneme represented by it. He was shown how to form the sound correctly. Joshua was required to repeat the sound made by the letter and he was then provided with opportunities to write the sound in the air, sand, water, soil and on the palm of his hand. Joshua was required to say the sound at the same time as writing the letter. A range of resources were used to reinforce the learning that was taking place. In one memorable lesson Joshua enjoyed making letters out of melted chocolate. After five months on the intervention, Joshua was able to identify all phonemes for all the letters of the alphabet and he also knew the phonemes for some digraphs.

REFLECTIVE TASK

- Why do you think Joshua found it difficult to master the simple alphabetic code?
- Why do you think the strategies worked?
- What are the next steps for Joshua?
- How might the practitioner work with Joshua to achieve these?

RESEARCH SUMMARY RESEARCH SUMMARY **RESEARCH SUMMARY** RESEARCH SUMMARY

Snowling, M.J. and Hulme, C. (2006), 'Language Skills, learning to read and reading intervention', *London Review of Education,* 4 (1), 63–76.
This paper argues that speech-processing impairments or broader language processing impairments can result in reading difficulties. Therefore the paper suggests that speech and language skills determine outcomes in reading.

A SUMMARY OF **KEY POINTS**

> Dyslexia is now seen to arise as a result of a core phonological deficit rather than a visual deficit.

> Learners with dyslexia may have low levels of self-esteem. This can increase after the initial diagnosis. Teachers need to preserve the child's self-esteem by being understanding and sympathetic. Above all, children with dyslexia need an empathetic teacher.

> All learners will benefit from multi-sensory approaches when being introduced to sound–symbol relationships. In addition, learners with dyslexia will benefit from a highly structured, multi-sensory phonics programme which builds in frequent opportunities for assessment.

MOVING *ON* > > > > > > MOVING *ON* > > > > > > MOVING *ON*

Now that you understand the importance of multi-sensory approaches for supporting learners with dyslexia, produce a set of multi-sensory graphemes that you will be able to use during your teaching career to support learners with dyslexia.

REFERENCES REFERENCES **REFERENCES** REFERENCES **REFERENCES** REFERENCES

Bradley, L. and Bryant, P. (1983) '"Categorising sound and learning to read": A causal connection nature', in Riddick, B. (1995) 'Dyslexia: dispelling the myths', *Disability and Society,* 10 (4), 457–473.

British Psychological Society (1999) cited in Hall, W. (2009), *Dyslexia in the Primary Classroom.* Exeter: Learning Matters.

Broomfield, H. and Combley, M. (2003), *Overcoming Dyslexia: A practical handbook for the classroom.* (2nd edn). London: Whurr.

Department for Education and Skills (2004) *Removing Barriers to Achievement: The Government Strategy for SEN.* Nottingham: DfES.

Edwards J. (1994) *The Scars of Dyslexia: Eight Case Studies in Emotional Reactions.* London: Cassell.

Frith, U. (1985) 'Beneath the surface of developmental dyslexia', in K. Patterson, M. Coltheart and J. Marshall (eds) *Surface Dyslexia*, pp.301–330, London: Routledge and Kegan Paul.

Gurney P.W. (1988) *Self-Esteem in Children with Special Educational Needs.* London and New York: Routledge.

Glazzard, J. (2004) *'A discussion of the factors which affect dyslexic pupils' self-esteem and the need for an early diagnosis',* Unpublished MA thesis, University of Sheffield.

Hall, W. (2009) *Dyslexia in the Primary Classroom.* Exeter: Learning Matters.

Humphrey, N. (2001) *'Self-Concept and Self-Esteem in Developmental Dyslexia: Implications for Teaching and Learning, Liverpool John Moores University: Unpublished PhD manuscript*, cited in Humphrey N. (2003) 'Facilitating a positive sense of self in pupils with Dyslexia: The role of Teachers and Peers', *Support for Learning*, 18 (3), 130–136.

Humphrey, N. (2002) 'Teacher and pupil ratings of self-esteem in developmental dyslexia', *British Journal of Special Education*, 29 (1), 29–36.

Humphrey, N. (2003) 'Facilitating a positive sense of self in pupils with dyslexia: The role of teachers and peers', *Support for Learning*, 18 (3), 130–136.

Humphrey, N. and Mullins, P.M. (2002) 'Self concept and self-esteem in developmental dyslexia', *Journal of Research in Special Educational Needs* 2 (2). **www.nasen.uk.com/e-journal**.

Lawrence, D. (1996) *Enhancing Self-Esteem in the Classroom* London: Paul Chapman.

Lowenstein, L. (1989) cited in Hall, W. (2009) *Dyslexia in the Primary Classroom.* Exeter: Learning Matters.

Manis, F.R., Seidenberg, M.S., Doi, L.M., McBride-Chang, C. and Peterson, A. (1996) 'On the basis of two sub-types of developmental dyslexia cognition', 58, 157–195 (in Coltheart, M. and Jackson,

N.E. (1998) 'Defining dyslexia', *Child Psychology and Psychiatry Review*, (3) 1, 12–16).

Miles T.R. and Miles, E. (1990) *Dyslexia: A Hundred Years On*. Milton Keynes and Philadelphia: Open University Press.

Riddick, B. (1995) 'Dyslexia: dispelling the myths', *Disability and Society*, 10 (4), 457–473.

Riddick B (1996) *Living With Dyslexia*. London and New York: Routledge.

Rose, J. (2006) *Independent Review of the Teaching of Early Reading: Final Report*. Department for Education and Skills.

Schumacher, J., Hoffmann, P., Schmal, C., Schulte-Korne, G. and Nothen, M (2007) 'Genetics of dyslexia: the evolving landscape', *Journal of Medical Genetics*, 44, 289–97, in Hall, W. (2009), *Dyslexia in the Primary Classroom*. Exeter: Learning Matters.

Shankweiler, D. and Crain, S. (1986) 'Language mechanisms and reading disorder: a modular approach', *Cognition*, 24, 139–164.

Share, D.L. (1995) 'Phonological recoding and self-teaching: Sine qua non of reading acquisition', *Cognition*, 55, 151–218.

Snowling, M. (1995) 'Phonological processing and developmental dyslexia', *Journal of Research in Reading*, 18, 132–138.

Snowling, M. (1998) 'Dyslexia as a phonological deficit: evidence and implications', *Child Psychology and Psychiatry Review*, 3 (1), 4–11.

Stanovich, K.E. (1986) 'Cognitive processes and the reading problems of learning disabled children: Evaluating the assumption of specificity', in Snowling, M. (1998), 'Dyslexia as a phonological deficit: evidence and implications', *Child Psychology and Psychiatry Review*, 3 (1), 4–11.

Stanovich, K.E. (1988) 'Explaining the differences between the dyslexic and the garden variety poor reader: The phonological-core-variable-difference model', *Journal of Learning Disabilities*, 21, 590–612.

Stanovich, K., Siegel, L.S., and Gottardo, A. (1997) 'Progress in the search for dyslexia subtypes, in Snowling, M. (1998), 'Dyslexia as a phonological deficit: evidence and implications', *Child Psychology and Psychiatry Review*, 3 (1), 4–11.

Stanovich, K.E and Stanovich, P.J. (1997) 'Further thoughts on aptitude/achievement discrepancy', *Educational Psychology in Practice*, 13 (1) 3–8.

Stein, J. and Walsh, V. (1997) cited in Hall, W. (2009) *Dyslexia in the Primary Classroom*. Exeter: Learning Matters.

Swann, W. (1985) Dyslexia Unit 25 Block 4 (E206): Personality, Development and Learning. Milton Keynes: Open University Press (in Riddick, B. (1996) *Living With Dyslexia*. London and New York: Routledge).

Taipale, M., Kaminen, N., Nopola-Hemmi, J., Haltia, T., Myllyluoma, B., Lyytinien, H., Muller, K., Kaaranen, M., Lindsberg, P., Hannula-Jouppi, K. and Kere, J. (2003) 'A candidate gene for developmental dyslexia encodes a nuclear tetratricopeptide repeat domain protein dynamically regulated in brain', *Proceedings of National Academy of Sciences of United States of America*, 30 September 2003, 100 (20), 11553–8, cited in Hall, W. (2009), *Dyslexia in the Primary Classroom*. Exeter: Learning Matters.

Turner, M. (1997) *Psychological Assessment of Dyslexia*. London: Whurr.

TDA (2008) *Special Educational Needs and/or Disabilities: A training resource for initial teacher training providers: primary undergraduate courses*. TDA.

FURTHER READING FURTHER READING **FURTHER READING** FURTHER READING

Pollock, J. and Waller, E. (2001) *Day to day dyslexia in the classroom*. Abingdon: RoutledgeFalmer.

Useful website

www.dyslexiaaction.org.uk/

5
Speech and language

Chapter objectives

This chapter will enable you to:

- understand the elements of language;
- understand the importance of monitoring speech, language and communication development;
- understand the foundations of effective communication in the classroom;
- recognise the possible impact of SEN on different aspects of language development;
- differentiate lesson preparation for pupils with speech, language and communication needs (SLCN) including those with English as an additional language;
- differentiate your questioning in class;
- model good communication, and support the development of storytelling in the classroom.

This chapter addresses the following Professional Standards for the award of QTS:

Q1, Q14, Q19, Q26, Q30, Q31

Introduction

> Language is what differentiates mankind from all other species. It is an extraordinary system of communication, making use of symbols, words, and a complex range of sounds. Societies have evolved many different languages. Each language uses a different set of symbols, stringing them together in different ways (grammar), and using different sound ranges (speech) and, for languages that are not oral, different signs on paper.

> (Penn, 2008, 58)

REFLECTIVE TASK

Think through the language you have engaged in today, for example speech, signs, reading, writing and thought.

What was the purpose of these engagements?

What would have been the effects of not having language on your powers to communicate?

Language and communication

Language is essential to the human species, and understanding how it is acquired and how it develops is very significant for teachers, especially when considering how to support children with special educational needs where the difficulty relates to speech, language and communication.

The SEN Code of Practice (DFES, 2001) says: *Most children with special educational needs have strengths and difficulties in one, some or all of the areas of speech, language and communication*.

The role of language

Jean Piaget's studies of child development concluded that a child acquired language as if by magic once the child reached a certain stage in their development. However, the work of Vygotsky on cognitive development suggests that language development is an interaction between the environment and the pupil's cognitive skills. It does not occur in a vacuum, but:

- develops in a sociocultural context;
- is influenced by the cognitive skills pupils bring with them;
- develops gradually and at varying rates.

Vygotsky describes a process where communication develops through social interaction with others and suggests that thought evolves separately and at a later stage of cognitive development (Jarvis, 2005). This suggests that it is only later that language becomes internalised, allowing the child to manipulate ideas mentally and follow instructions from others. The implication of this has a major significance for children whose special needs involve any kind of speech and language difficulties as their ability to internalise information may be severely compromised. Individual Education Plans need to recognise this and offer support accordingly, as described later in this chapter.

Making sense of language

When children first begin to speak they react to the environment around them. Initially this means single words and this is followed by two or more words which may appear to the listener to be unconnected. Many researchers such as Chomsky (1950), Skinner (1957) and Crystal (1976) have attempted to find a pattern for early language acquisition but there is still work to be done to fully understand how children's language develops. One element that appears to remain constant in all communities is that communication with young children is delivered at a slower pace than adult conversations, vocabulary is often repetitive and simple, the intonation is exaggerated and the grammatical structure is simpler.

Non-verbal communication

What is clear is that children do manage to make themselves understood to their parents or those closest to them. This may be made easier by contextual clues such as where the child is looking, facial expression, tone of voice or body movements (Wood, 1998). For children with specific educational needs such as austistic spectrum disorders there are problems 'reading' such non-verbal signals as they are not recognised as interpretive clues to meaning. Similarly, some children with a visual impairment may have limited experience of using and seeing non-verbal communication.

The elements of language

Frederickson and Cline (2009) define effective communication as recognising the forms of a shared language in an interactive manner that conveys meaning.

- They know the forms of language they share – how the words sound and how they go together (competence in phonology and syntax).
- They are able to use those forms to convey meaning and can understand what others mean when they use them (competence in semantics).
- They understand the social conventions that determine how people use language to each other, so that they appreciate another speaker's intentions in speaking and can communicate their own intentions to a listener (pragmatic competence).
- They can vary their style of communication and the language they use to suit the needs of different listeners in a conversation (conversational competence).
- They understand how language conventions vary with the social and cultural context (sociolinguistic competence).

(Frederickson and Cline, 2009, 240)

The cycle of interaction

Tassoni (2003) identifies a cycle of interaction, which is based on seven stages and describes some of the difficulties that may be encountered at each stage. This cycle relates to all children but Tassoni elaborates how children with speech and language difficulties may struggle to communicate at each stage. It is a very useful model that will help you to identify precisely the area of difficulty a child with speech and language issues may be experiencing.

Stage 1   Information

The sender has to decide what they want to convey.
Difficulties: Children may not be able to process their thoughts and feelings.

Stage 2   Encoding

The sender chooses a medium in which to send their message. This can be using spoken language, written, non-verbal or visual.
Difficulties: Children may not be able to choose a medium that is appropriate, e.g. they may throw an object rather than use words or a gesture to show their feelings. Children may also have difficulties in encoding information using words because words are abstract symbols. Children may not have the vocabulary to put their thoughts into words.

Stage 3   Transfer of information

At this point the information is sent out.

Stage 4   Reception of information

The receiver now hears or takes in the information.
Difficulties: Children may not be able to see the gestures or fully hear the sounds. Children may not be able to read what has been written. Children may not be able to remember what is being said.

Stage 5   Decoding the information

The information is now interpreted.

Difficulties: Children may not have the receptive vocabulary to understand the meaning. Children may not be able to understand the gesture or tone of voice. Children may not be able to process the information effectively.

Stage 6   Feedback

The receiver of the information may show some reaction. Sometimes the sender of the information may not see the feedback, e.g. if a letter is sent.

Difficulties: Children may not be able to show appropriate feedback; they may laugh or smile when the message sent is sad or serious.

Stage 7   Response

They may then wish to send information themselves, in which case the cycle continues.

Difficulties: Children may not be able to respond to others in way that can be understood or they may need plenty of time.

(Tassoni, 2003, 105)

Expressive and receptive communication

Where pupils with SEN use alternative forms of communication, such as signing rather than oral language, we use the terms 'expressive and receptive communication' rather than 'speaking and listening'.

This form of communication can manifest itself in a variety of forms. Blakemore and Frith (2005) refer to studies undertaken by Laura-Ann Petitto and colleagues (2004) at McGill University in Toronto where deaf babies were observed to engage in 'babbling with their hands' in a similar manner to hearing babies who babble using their voices.

Conventionally children with speech and communication problems often use signing for communication or as an aid to communication and this can enable them to be more actively included in their community. However, it has been the author's experience that some parents of deaf children prefer to avoid their children learning to sign as they are concerned that reliance on this means of communication can limit social interaction with the hearing community and increase their child's isolation. Conversely, some parents only want their child to sign, believing that their child will be happier remaining in a smaller supportive non-hearing community.

You should be aware that there are a number of different types of signing. The most commonly used in this country are British Sign Language (BSL), which involves finger spelling, and Makaton, which uses symbols for whole words or actions.

The third commonly used form of expressive communication employs interactive media such as specially adapted computer keyboards to create an artificial 'voice' for the individual.

Language and diversity (children with English as an additional language – EAL)

One aspect that you need to take into account when determining if a child has a speech and language difficulty is whether English is the child's second language.

The Education Act 1996 is clear on this point:

> *A child is not to be taken as having a learning difficulty solely because the language (or form of language) in which he is, or will be, taught is different from a language (or form of language) which has at any time been spoken in his home.*
>
> (Education Act 1996, Section 312)

In practice this means that you must take into account whether the difficulty the child is experiencing with language is based upon his or her lack of opportunity to hear and use the forms and conventions of the English language, or whether it is related to cognitive development. Similarly, you need to determine whether the child is learning two languages at once and becoming confused between differing grammatical and/or syntactical structures.

Problems associated with the development of communication skills

You can expect to encounter some or any of the problems listed below while on placement and throughout your teaching career. Some are more prevalent than others and the degree of difficulty for an individual child will also be very variable. This list is not exhaustive but covers the most common problems that may impact upon speech and language development.

Hearing problems

Children who have a permanent hearing loss are likely to have been diagnosed as such before entering school. They may have hearing aids or even cochlear implants. In most cases they will have some support as part of their schooling and you will be able to ask for advice from the Special Educational Needs Co-ordinator to understand their difficulties.

However, children whose hearing problems are less severe are often not identified at birth and can go undetected for some time. It is estimated that as many as one in four children in a Reception class may have a mild or slight hearing loss (Tassoni, 2003). Children who are prone to heavy colds and coughs can experience a mild conductive hearing loss which fluctuates. The reason for this is that the eustachian tube which connects the nose and the ear becomes blocked, causing sound to be distorted. The case study below illustrates the signs you need to look for.

CASE STUDY
A fluctuating hearing loss

Mary, a child in a Reception class, often suffered from colds and a runny nose. When she had such symptoms Mary seemed to spend a great deal of time playing by herself. She had difficulty following instructions and often looked confused. She didn't appear able to settle in whole-class situations and didn't engage in groups discussions. Her speech could appear muffled or indistinct. The class teacher suspected that Mary might have a fluctuating hearing loss. she talked to Mary's mother and they agreed that a visit to the family doctor would be made the next time Mary's symptoms reoccurred. The school would also arrange for the school nurse to conduct a hearing test using specialist equipment. These actions indicated that Mary did have a fluctuating hearing loss and a hospital appointment was made, where a full range of tests confirmed the

---

diagnosis. Mary's ears were fitted with gromits to drain the fluid from her ears more effectively. Her class teachers ensured that Mary always sat facing people who were talking to her, and that they spoke clearly.

Visual impairment

Children with an undetected visual impairment may peer or frown intently when looking at objects, books, pictures or posters, holding them very closely to their face. They often appear clumsy and accident-prone. If you come across a child with these difficulties, share your concern with the class teacher and/or the SENCO.

Children who have an identified serious visual impairment may not have the visual non-verbal clues to associate spoken language with the material world and often take longer to acquire vocabulary.

Other physical impairments

Some children are born with facial disorders such as cleft palate or what is commonly referred to as being 'tongue-tied', where the skin under the tongue prevents the child from being able to communicate effectively. These problems rarely stop the child from communicating, but their ability to produce certain sounds may be affected. These issues are usually picked up by health visitors before a child starts nursery or school and a referral made to a speech therapist.

Down's syndrome

Down's syndrome is a learning disability. Children are born with the condition and it can be mild or very severe. Many children with Down's syndrome can cope very well in mainstream schools but some may experience difficulties when using speech and language. Their speech may appear slurred, especially if they are tired, and some may experience difficulties with their vision and/or their cognitive development.

Neurological problems

Some children are born with central nervous system disorders such as cerebral palsy. This affects the muscles and can result in involuntary muscle contractions which may affect their speech. Again it is likely that they will already have been referred to a speech therapist before starting school.

Autistic spectrum disorders

There is still much to be discovered about autistic spectrum disorders. The two main types were identified in the 1940s and are called Kanner's syndrome and Asperger syndrome. Further information on autism can be found in Chapter 6, 'Supporting children with autistic spectrum disorder'. Children may not be diagnosed as having autistic spectrum disorders for some time as the signs are not always immediately obvious; indeed some adults can discover they have Asperger syndrome. The reason why it can be difficult to detect is that many of the signs are also indicative of other problems. The main impairments to look out for are problems with social interaction, social communication and imagination.

Lorna Wing and Judith Gould (1979) carried out a survey of children living in Camberwell, an area of south London. From this they identified the Triad of Impairments which can be used to define identify an autistic spectrum disorder. These are:

- social impairment;
- verbal and non-verbal language impairment;
- repetitive/stereotyped activities.

Although some children with autism may have language, all children on the autistic spectrum fundamentally have problems with communication, which is different from language. They struggle to understand the purpose of communication in terms of the back and forth of exchanges and the rules of engagement.

For some children commercial resources such as Picture Exchange Communication Systems (PECS) can be very beneficial. Refer to Chapter 6 for further information about strategies to support learners with autistic spectrum disorder.

A child with autistic spectrum disorder is likely to have difficulty recognising and imagining the feelings of others, and children with Asperger syndrome often want to join in with others but may display inappropriate behaviour, such as punching, when doing so. They can find it difficult to engage in social conversations. On the one hand they may find talking very difficult, while on the other they may repeat phrases (echolalia) they have heard over and over again, or use inappropriate vocabulary. Their imagination is often limited and they may become very attached to unusual play items such as household appliances. Above all, children with autism do not adapt well to changes in their routine as they find it difficult to predict what is going to happen to them next.

CASE STUDY
Tom's journey
Tom was diagnosed as having Asperger syndrome in Year 2. He was given a statement of special educational need which gave him access to a teaching assistant for 15 hours a week. Tom was very vocal in class but often appeared not to be listening. He would make loud squawking noises while the teacher was talking to the class, which was very distracting. Tom was very good at maths and would always shout out the answers or oral questions, not allowing others have their turn. He took all statements very literally; for example, when the class was told to 'pull up your socks' he would follow the instruction to the letter. As Tom got older he began to be fascinated by writing. He would write very literal stories which were peppered with his own comments on his writing always enclosed in square brackets. He used unusual vocabulary which was often far in advance of his years and was sometimes inappropriate to the context. Children found him difficult to play with in the playground as he would want to join in on his terms and 'wind-milled' his limbs in a very forceful manner. He would often complain that children hurt him, but could not recognise when he had hurt them. Tom also had a strong fascination for computers which at times became an issue when he redesigned access codes for the school network.

The school used a variety of strategies including one-to-one, group sessions and lunchtime support. At times Tom was able to go home for lunch on days when his mother was not at work. Parents of other children were aware that Tom had difficulties socialising and in the main were supportive and understanding. When Tom transferred to high school he was allowed to move classes five minutes before the end of lessons to give him the chance to relocate away from the crowd.

REFLECTIVE TASK
REFLECTIVE TASK

How would you organise Tom's support time to be most effective?
What would you include in his IEP?

Emotional and social difficulties

Some children acquire early language skills but are unable to apply them because of emotional or social difficulties. One form of this is selective mutism. Children with this problem tend to communicate well in certain situations and environments but choose not to communicate in others. This occurs most commonly when a child leaves the family home for the first time and enters school and refuses to communicate with the teacher and/or their peers. The most effective strategies to deal with this issue have centred on the parents working with the child on school tasks in the classroom after the school day and the gradual withdrawal of their input over a long period of time, or the use of pictorial communication systems can be effective.

The impact of social environments

The home environment significantly impacts on the development of children's speech, language and communication. Children learn to communicate by listening to and imitating the world around them. If the child does not have access to this s/he is likely to experience speech and language difficulties.

It has been found that children who came from homes where the parents left school at the minimum age and without educational qualifications used less complex language and had significant differences in measured intelligences by the age of seven than their counterparts from homes where at least one parent had benefited from extended education. It was also true that school experiences did not eradicate these differences (Tough, 1977). The impact on children with SLCN is particularly pronounced. The development of Sure Start and children's centres is starting to improve the situation, but you may still find children in your school who have not had the benefit of such interventions.

Many people are also concerned about the influence of virtual technologies on children's development of language. Children entering school do seem to be less advanced in SLC than in the past. At this time much of this is anecdotal and based upon reports from head-teachers. However, recent research conducted by Gross (2009) in middle-class households suggests that one in five boys (22 per cent) and one in seven girls (13 per cent) have trouble learning to talk, and that 40 families out of 1000 polled reported that their child had not spoken until the age of three years. Gross reports that half the families surveyed had the television on for half the time and that, in this situation, the amount of time adults talk to young children falls away to almost nothing. She does add a note of caution that some children are late talkers, but recommends that advice be sought if a child shows no signs of talking by the age of two.

The role of the speech and language therapist

Access to a speech and language therapist is very much dependent upon local availability. Baird, in Norbury (2008), cites her unpublished data for UK (checklist for autism) in the South East of England stating that 8.4 per cent of children up to the age of three years had been referred to a speech and language therapist, while in areas of social deprivation the figure was as high as 14.6 per cent.

Although there is screening for sight and hearing loss, currently there is no formal national health screening for speech and language problems in pre-school children and the onus rests with the primary care practitioner to make a referral.

It is the role of the primary care practitioner to establish the nature of any parental or other professional concerns, to assess the type and impact of the speech and/or language problem, its severity and whether there are other developmental or social/emotional issues. They then decide whether the problem needs monitoring to see how it develops, who needs active treatment, whose needs are more complex due to additional problems, or whether there is no significant problem.

The assessment of speech and language

Standardised tests do exist for speech and language therapists to establish that a child has a particular problem. One which is regularly used for pre-school children is the *Bus Story* (Renfrew, 1991). This involves the adult telling a story with pictures to the child, then the child retelling the story to the adult. It is considered to be a good guide to overall language competence and a good indicator of long-term language functioning (Bishop and Edmundson, 1987). When a child is referred for speech and language assessment a hearing test is mandatory, as is a contextual history of the child's communication and behaviour in the home. Other major considerations include whether there are other developmental issues and the access to a good communicative environment.

Developing a communicative environment in the classroom and some core skills of teacher communication

The key to developing a communicative environment that impacts on children with SLCN lies more in the nature of the strategies used rather than merely the amount of resources applied, according to the report of the Office of Her Majesty's Chief Inspector (2006), which concludes that:

> The provision of additional resources to pupils – such as support from teaching assistants – did not ensure good quality intervention or adequate progress by pupils. There was a misconception that provision of additional resources was the key requirement for individual pupils, whereas ... key factors for good progress were: the involvement of a specialist teacher; good assessment; work tailored to challenge pupils sufficiently; and commitment from school leaders to ensure good progress for all pupils.
>
> (HMI, 2006, 2)

REFLECTIVE TASK

REFLECTIVE TASK

Consider the above statement in the light of your experience in placement schools.

Do you agree or disagree with the finding that additional resources were not always the key to progression?

Have you been able to observe the work of a specialist teacher?

If so, how effective was their involvement?

The strategies need to be consistent and progressive. Broadly speaking, a little and often is likely to achieve the best results. The pedagogy should follow a structure similar to the following.

- Provide opportunities for communication to take place.
- Wherever possible give instructions in short sentences or phrases and, where appropriate, use a series of instructions presented in pictures so the child knows what to do.
- The learning and embedding of concepts need frequent reinforcement and lots of practice.
- Feedback from completed tasks needs to be immediate, explicit and oral wherever possible.
- Formative assessment should inform the next step for learning.
- All tasks should be planned using small and discrete steps with clear short-term objectives.
- The involvement of a specialist teacher should be actively sought and encouraged.
- Visual learning.

As practitioners, what opportunities for communication should you be aiming to develop?

Firstly, ensure that you have the child's attention. This may seem obvious, but when talking to the child, refer to the child by name and get eye contact before proceeding with your conversation. For example, *Ben... what do you think about this story?* rather than *What do you think of this story, Ben?*

By organising your communication in this way you help the child to recognise that you are directing your question at him/her.

Give the child time to consider their response; do not jump in too quickly. If necessary, repeat the question and continue to give them thinking time. Wood (2003) observes:

> What appears to be the dominant teaching register, involving frequent teacher-directed questions, may be effective in achieving certain managerial and instructional ends, but it seems unlikely to provide good conditions for developing children's powers as narrators, informants and, perhaps, self-regulating learners.
>
> (Wood, 2003, 179)

Tassoni (2003) describes the optimum conditions for language learning to be a language partner rather than a teacher. In order to achieve this you will need to:

- make good eye contact with the child;

- smile and display pleasure when the child tries to involve you;
- adapt your conversational style, making it more of a dialogue than an instruction;
- give the child time to reflect;
- value non-verbal communications;
- avoid rushed conversations.

PRACTICAL TASK PRACTICAL TASK **PRACTICAL TASK** PRACTICAL TASK **PRACTICAL TASK**

Consider the two conversations below.
Which of them provides the most opportunity for children to develop their speech and language skills?

CASE STUDY
Asking the right questions
Conversation 1
Adult: What you have been making?
Child: A farm.
Adult: I like this cow. What colour is it?
Child: It's brown.
Adult: That's right. Are all cows brown?
Child: I think so.
Adult: Why don't you see if there are any other cows in the box, they may be different colours? I'll come back later to see what you have found out.

Conversation 2
Adult: Hello William. Can I come and play with your farm too, it looks very interesting. I like the hens best because they make a clucking sound. Which one is your favourite animal?
Child: This one [picking up a pig].
Adult: Yes I like pigs too. I wonder where pigs live on the farm?
Child: Here [pointing to a muddy field on the playmat].
Adult: What a lovely place to live. The mud must be very squelchy. Shall we pretend to be pigs in a muddy field and stomp about in the mud?

In the first conversation the adult is using closed questioning that limits the child's opportunity to expand on his/her answers. In the second conversation the child is encouraged to be a talk partner.

It follows that it is good practice to monitor how much opportunity you provide for the children to talk to you in your teaching, rather than the children always listening to you.

All teaching spaces should be language-rich environments and this is no different for children with SLCN. They enjoy taking part in songs, rhymes and action games and should be encouraged to join in whenever possible, including using signing if appropriate to their needs. For example, many schools now include signing when singing in assembly whether or not they have children who rely upon this means of communication, not only to acknowledge diversity, but also as a way of helping all the children to think more carefully about the words they are singing.

You will need to consider the complexity of the language you use with children who have SLCN. They will become disinterested in talking to you if they find it difficult to interpret your conversation. We discussed earlier in the chapter that adults naturally repeat and emphasise key words in a sentence with young children and this continues to be a useful strategy for older children with SLCN.

Children with SLCN need a relaxed atmosphere in which to learn. One of the best ways to achieve this is developing language through play. The Early Years Foundation Stage framework (DfES, 2007) is based around play and it may well be appropriate to continue to use some of this methodology for older children in some of their learning. It allows the adult to move in to encourage new vocabulary then move out to allow the child to practise this new learning alongside their peers. It also stimulates the imagination in a non-threatening manner.

Some physical aspects of the classroom environment can make it difficult for children with SLCN to communicate. This is especially true if a child has a hearing or visual impairment. Try to avoid standing with your back towards a bright light such as a window or display screen. Your face is then in shadow and a child who relies on your face for visual clues to grasp the full meaning of your conversation will struggle to fully comprehend you. Similarly, do not keep the room too dark for your face to be clearly visible, and do not engage children in conversation when you have your back to them. Whenever possible, ensure that the classroom environment is free from echoes. This can be achieved by having curtained windows and carpeted floors. It is an interesting fact that children with hearing impairments are generally at least twice as good at lip reading than their hearing peers.

You can also employ visual aids to support the development of communication, such as puppets and pictures or objects that relate to the teaching objective of the lesson.

Much of the above reflects good educational practice for all children, but it is especially important for children with SLCN.

Narrative development

The following account of how children develop the skills of spoken narrative is quoted from the SEN resource for Initial Teacher Training (TDA, 2008). Children with SLCN may take longer to reach each developmental point than other children, but the continuum remains the same.

In terms of the type of narrative which appears earlier in development, pupils seem to find routine accounts the easiest to produce in sequence. On the other hand, at the very beginning of language development, children tend to mention events that are noticeable and extraordinary, rather than ordinary events. The origin of story lies in the moment when an infant notices that something has happened, and draws your attention to it (about nine months in typical development). There is a close relationship between overall linguistic skill and narrative ability. Three- and four-year-olds who are syntactically advanced produce longer and more complex narratives than children who are syntactically delayed. The ability to put two or three words together appears to be a significant milestone in narrative development – at this level, children find it difficult to produce extended sequences of narrative.

From about nine months onwards children show you that something interesting has happened, by vocalising, pointing, looking at it, and looking at you. This develops until by around 12 months when children make reference to an immediately past event, e.g. by pointing to the mixer, rotating a hand and saying 'Rrr' when it had just finished working.

Children begin to make reference to past events, and can participate in narrative when this is scaffolded by an adult at about two years of age. At first, they mention one event, usually something that has happened recently. They begin to order events temporally. Narratives are a strong feature in adult–child interchanges from this point on. They can respond to questions and prompts about what happened.

By three years, six months, children are able to refer to place ('Where'), but are poor on person ('Who'). At first, events may not be in sequence, and information may be left out. This becomes more complete as children get older. A lot of effect is used in narrative. They are beginning to use conjunctions appropriately to join up the narrative. 'Chaining' begins: a sequence of chronological actions which are causally linked, but without any evidence of intentions or goals, And then... and then...

Between the ages of five and six years children regularly include 'setting' statements (when and where the event happened), and begin to organise stories around a central problem or conflict involving a progression of events: a problem, an initiating event and consequences.

There is awareness of immediate future and stock characteristics associated with scripts, for example, heroes and villains in fairy stories. Understanding of basic emotions is shown: anger, joy, fear, sadness. Cause and effect relationships are evident. Story structures emerge. By the age of six, children can produce complete structured narratives.

Stories become more elaborate, with multiple episodes, and represent more than one point of view between the ages of six and nine years. There is:

- awareness that people change as a result of what happens to them;
- awareness of distinction between appearance and reality (deceit and trickery);
- awareness of multiple meanings;
- distinction between literal and figurative language;
- insight into complex relationships between characters and context, leading to unpredictable events;
- understanding of the need to provide explanations for events and behaviour;
- understanding of more complex emotions – jealousy, guilt;
- understanding of timeframes – days, weeks, etc.

Narrative skills continue to develop throughout childhood, and the number of complete episodes increases up to the age of about 16.

(TDA, 2008)

Support and differentiation for pupils with SLCN

Throughout this chapter we have emphasised that children with SLCN require the same if not more access to language as other children. The difference lies in the way this access is provided. Children with SLCN need more one-to-one and small-group teaching than their peers which may be enhanced by the presence of some support within the classroom. This may take the form of a specialist teacher or a suitably trained education teaching assistant. Nevertheless it is you, as the class teacher, who must plan and prepare lessons that are differentiated according to the needs of all the children in your class. The first action you need to take is to become familiar with the specific needs of the child in your class who has SLCN difficulties. This is not simply knowing what the problems are, but identifying the next steps of learning for the child. They will need more time to understand and practise new vocabulary and concepts. It may be useful for them to have been given time in advance of your lesson to introduce this to them. This will allow them to concentrate upon the content and your delivery rather than having to make sense of the vocabulary simultaneously. Your daily planning needs to detail how you will ensure this takes place.

A SUMMARY OF **KEY POINTS**

> This chapter has explored some of the main issues around the acquisition of speech and language, its importance as a means of communication and as a tool for thinking.

> It has described how language is constructed in our society and how this may be different to how it is constructed in other communities, which may impact on children with EAL.

> Effective communication in the classroom has been explored and suggestions made as to how this may be used to differentiate the language learning for children with SLCN, including the use of effective questioning.

> We have examined how a range of SLCN difficulties can impact on language development and suggested some strategies you may be able to employ to aid the language learning of these children.

MOVING *ON* > > > > > > MOVING *ON* > > > > > > MOVING *ON*

If you are not familiar with signing, watch some children's television which provides signing alongside the programme. Try turning off the sound and following the programme without oral clues. This may provide you with useful insight into the difficulties that may be encountered by a child with a hearing loss.

On your next placement, investigate the support given to a child with SLCN. What is the nature of their difficulty? When was it discovered? What support have the child and its family received from the primary care practitioners and the school?

REFERENCES REFERENCES **REFERENCES** REFERENCES **REFERENCES** REFERENCES

Baird, G. in Norbury, C.F., Tomblin, J.B. and Bishop, D.V.M. (eds) (2008) *Understanding Developmental Language Disorders*. Hove: Psychology Press.

Blakemore, S-J. and Frith, U. (2005) *The learning brain*. Oxford: Blackwell.

Crystal, D. (1976) *Child Language, Learning and Linguistics*. London: Edward Arnold.

Department for Education and Skills (2001) Special Educational Needs Code of Practice, Ref. DfES/581/2001. London: DfES.

Department for Education and Skills (2003) *Every Child Matters*. Norwich: TSO.

Dockerell, J.E. and Lindsay, G., in Norbury, C.F., Tomblin, J.B. and Bishop, D.V.M. (eds) (2008) *Understanding Developmental Language Disorders*. Hove: Psychology Press.

Frederickson, N. and Cline, T. (2009) *Special Educational Needs, Inclusion and Diversity*, 2nd edition. Maidenhead: Open University Press.

Gross, J. (2010) 'The language barrier', quoted in *The Sunday Times* 10.01.2010 article by Griffiths, S. (p9).

Jarvis, M. (2005) *The psychology of effective teaching and learning*. Cheltenham: Nelson Thornes.

Office of Her Majesty's Chief Inspector (2006) *The Annual Report of Her Majesty's Chief Inspector of Schools 2004/5*. London: Ofsted.

Penn, H. (2008) *Understanding Early Childhood Issues and Controversies*, 2nd edition. Maidenhead: Open University Press.

Renfrew, C. (1991) *Renfrew Bus Story Manual: A Test of Narrative Speech*. Oxford: Winslow.

Skinner, B. F. (1957) *Verbal Behavior*. London: Methuen.

Tassoni, P. (2003) *Supporting Special Needs. Understanding Inclusion in the Early Years*. Oxford: Heinemann.

TDA (2008) *Special Educational Needs and/or Disabilities: A training resource for initial teacher training providers: primary undergraduate courses.* TDA.

Tough, J. (1977) *The Development of Meaning*. Oxford: Wiley.

Wing, L. and Gould, J. (1974) 'Severe impairments of social interaction and associated abnormalities in children. Epidemiology and classification', *Journal of Autism and Childhood Schizophrenia*, 9, 11–29.

Wood, D. (1998) *How Children Think and Learn*, 2nd edition. Oxford: Blackwell.

FURTHER READING FURTHER READING **FURTHER READING** FURTHER READING

Garner, P. (2009) *Special Educational Needs. The Key Concepts*. Abingdon: Routledge.

Pugh, G. and Duffy, B. (eds) (2008) *Contemporary Issues in the Early Years*, 4th edition. London: Sage.

Useful websites

www.nationalstrategies.standards.dcsf.gov.uk EYFS Inclusion Development Programme (IDP): Speech, language and communication needs (SLCN) e-learning course.

www.ican.org.uk This charity supports children's communication and is a rich source of information.

6
Supporting children with autistic spectrum disorders

Chapter objectives

By the end of this chapter you should be aware of:

- the similarities and differences between autism and Asperger syndrome;
- the nature of autistic spectrum disorders (ASD) and the barriers to learning and participation for this group of learners, including knowledge of the triad of impairments;
- strategies that you can use in the classroom to support the learning of this group of children.

This chapter addresses the following Professional Standards for the award of QTS:

Q1, Q2, Q6, Q19

Introduction

Children with autism are often discussed as though they represent a homogenous group of learners. Strategies to support the learning and development of these children will need to be as diverse as the needs of each learner. Warnock (2005) has highlighted key issues associated with the inclusion of children with autism into mainstream learning environments. These concerns will be discussed in this chapter. However, it is likely that at some point during your career you will be responsible for the education of a child with autism and therefore it is crucial that you have a good understanding of how their needs can be met (Amaladoss, 2006). This chapter provides an overview of the evolution of the concept of autism and highlights the challenges faced by this diverse group. Practical strategies for supporting children with autism are discussed.

Autism and Asperger syndrome

The first references to 'early infantile autism' were made by the child psychiatrist Leo Kanner in 1943 (Kanner, 1943). Kanner noted the aloofness of people in this group and derived the term 'autism' from *auto* which is Greek for 'self'. Kanner and his colleague Leon Eisenberg identified specific criteria for diagnosing this condition. They identified that these children are typically aloof and indifferent to others and tended to develop repetitive routines (Kanner and Eisenberg, 1956, cited in Wing, 2007). Kanner noted the lack of social interaction as a defining characteristic of infantile autism and the existence of echolalia in some children, where words that had been heard were repeated. These children rarely had speech but in cases where speech did exist, none of the children used it as a tool for reciprocal conversation. Kanner believed that this pattern of behaviour was uncommon and quite distinct from all other childhood conditions (Wing, 2007). Kanner initially assumed that all children with this condition were fundamentally intelligent but developmentally delayed. However, this assumption was incorrect and it is now known that the majority of individuals with autism also appear to have additional, and often severe, learning difficulties (Jordan and Powell, 1995). Kanner initially thought that social impairment was present at birth and therefore part of an individual's biological make-up. He later rejected this idea and blamed parenting styles for this pattern of behaviour, although he subsequently dismissed this idea (Wing, 2007).

In 1944, Hans Asperger, a Viennese paediatrician, studied a small group of four boys at the University Paediatric Clinic in Vienna. Asperger described the characteristic features that these children had in common and how they differed from children with typical development. These children appeared to have average or above average levels of intelligence and good expressive language but their language skills were not utilised for two-way conversations. Asperger, like Kanner, also used the term 'autism' and it was only in 1981 that Lorna Wing introduced the term 'Asperger syndrome' to describe this group of individuals (TDA, 2008).

The triad of impairments

Lorna Wing used the term 'autistic spectrum disorder' (ASD) as a broad term for children who displayed common characteristics. Wing and Gould (1979) investigated the characteristics of children with autism. Their research identified the existence of a group of children who were socially impaired. This was consistent with the earlier findings of Kanner and his colleague. However, they also found that when social impairment was present, social communication and inflexibility of thought and behaviour were also present (Wing, 2007). They used the term *triad of impairments* (Wing, 1988) to describe the difficulties experienced by these children.

Social impairment

Social impairment is characteristic of all children with autistic spectrum disorder. Children with social impairment may have no interest in social interaction and they may display little interest in other people. They may be socially aloof and indifferent to strangers, although they may be more responsive to people who are familiar to them (Wing, 2007). They may reject approaches from others and may attempt to isolate themselves (Wing, 2007). As a trainee teacher you need to understand that there are degrees of social impairment. Social impairment lies on a continuum from those who are solitary and withdrawn (classic autism) to those who will respond passively when approached by others but will not initiate interaction themselves. At another end of the continuum may be those children who seek attention from others but often do not know how to deal with it (Jordan and Powell, 1995).

Children with social impairment may fail to grasp social rules. For example, they may not understand the need for one's own personal space. Socialising with others does not come naturally to children with autistic spectrum disorder. The company of others is not something they seek or desire. Social situations can be very stressful and they may have difficulty understanding the emotions and feelings of others. They may upset others as a result of failing to understand social codes of behaviour. They may avoid eye contact and find it distressing to make eye contact with others. This has implications for you as a trainee teacher. Never force a child with ASD to make eye contact with you. You will need to teach them explicitly about the effects of their actions on other people's feelings and you should therefore not label the child as 'naughty' or 'difficult'.

What are the implications of these difficulties for you as a trainee teacher? The first thing to remember is that children with autism may find social situations distressing or frightening. Do not force social contact and be sensitive to their needs. Social interactions need to be taught. You cannot assume that children with ASD will know how to behave in a group situation. Start slowly and gently encourage the child to tolerate simple social contact with others (Wing, 2007). Limit the time for social contact initially and limit the number of children in a group. This can be gradually increased as the child gains confidence. Develop positive relationships with parents or carers and plan strategies and interventions carefully in collaboration with them. It is possible that they may have chosen a mainstream placement as a way of helping their child to develop social interaction skills. You will need to develop a *deep empathy* (Wing, 2007, 27) for these children. After periods of focused social interaction, these children may need to go into their own quiet place for focused one-to-one teaching. They should be prepared for periods of social interaction, rather than interactions being forced on them. A highly ordered routine will be necessary so that children know what is going to happen at specific times during the day. Be aware that noisy environments may distress children with ASD and they may be particularly sensitive to bright lights. They may try to block out noise by putting their hands over their ears. Finally, you need to be calm when a child makes an accurate observation that offends. Children with autism need to be gradually taught the codes of appropriate social behaviour and they will need to be taught very explicitly about the way in which their actions can affect the feelings and emotions of others.

Language and communication

Children with ASD often have limited expressive language. Commonly, they do not understand the function of language as a tool for reciprocal conversation, and speech may only be used to satisfy a personal need or to talk about things of immediate interest to themselves (Wing, 2007). They may take the meaning of language literally and they may find it difficult to understand colloquial phrases. In addition, they may take sarcasm literally. Some children may have good vocabulary (particularly children with Asperger syndrome), although they may not use this vocabulary to engage in two-way conversations. They may echo words that they have heard and their comprehension of language may be weak. Some children may talk 'at' other people or even speak in different languages, thus demonstrating a failure to grasp the fundamental function of language as a tool for communication. Therefore, although speech may be developed, an understanding of speech as a tool for communication may be lacking. The extent of a child's difficulties with communication will lie on a continuum from those with no speech to those who have quite well-developed speech. Some children have excellent grammar and pronunciation and a talent for a foreign language (Jordan and Powell, 1995). However, poor communication remains a fundamental problem in all children with ASD. Many children with ASD do not understand facial expressions, expressive gestures and body postures (Jordan and Powell, 1995).

What are the implications of this for your classroom practice? Instructions may need to be accompanied by visual prompts or modelling. You will need to teach conversational skills such as listening, turn-taking and the value of sharing knowledge with others. You cannot assume that these skills will be secure. Think carefully about the way in which you phrase instructions. A simple request such as *can you draw a triangle?* is intended to elicit more than a reply of *yes* (Jordan, 2005). Tasks may need to be explained pictorially rather than through verbal instructions.

Rigidity of thought and behaviour

Children with ASD often develop rigid patterns of behaviour. They may repeat certain behaviours, such as dropping an object on a table repeatedly or spinning a coin. They may develop obsessions with a favourite object or they may become obsessed on cars, trains or motorbikes. Changes to familiar routines may cause distress and they may resist change. They may find imaginative play very difficult. Pretend play is often delayed or absent altogether (Jordan and Powell, 1995) and they may find it difficult to differentiate between reality and imagination. Creativity is often lacking.

As a trainee teacher you will need to ensure that the teaching day is very well structured. The use of a visual timetable (discussed below) will help the child to see what activities are scheduled during the day. Creative teachers can integrate the child's 'obsessions' into the daily schedule. If a child has a particular obsession with castles, you might wish to build in some time during the day when the child can build castles out of construction kits or read about castles in the book area. You might want to provide the child with opportunities to play a simulation game on the computer where the simulation is based inside a castle. The activities you provide will depend on the skills and interests of the child. If this time is scheduled on the daily timetable and the timetable is followed in order, you can then use this as a bargaining tool. For example, if number work comes before 'castles' on the daily schedule, you can teach the child that they must complete the first task before they can move on to their obsession. This becomes a 'rule' which the child learns to follow and helps to ensure that the child receives access to a broad and balanced curriculum. The best teachers will use children's obsessions and draw on these for curriculum planning purposes. However, children need to know that they cannot spend all their time engaging in their obsessions. Try to keep changes to the classroom layout to a minimum and warn children about any changes to the curriculum or the classroom systems, routines and classroom organisation. Slowly you should aim to introduce learners to new experiences and interests in order to give them access to a broad and rich curriculum.

Causes of autism

During the 1940s and 1950s it was thought that parental style was responsible for autism (Wing, 2007). However, later research in the 1960s confirmed that autism is caused by irregularities in brain development, often before birth (Wing, 1997). Strong evidence now confirms that genetic factors play a part in brain dysfunction (Bailey *et al.*, 1995; Jordan and Powell, 1995; Rutter, 1999). There is no single cause of autism but the evidence supports biological explanations. Autism is therefore explained as a product of nature rather than a product of nurture, although this does not exclude the possibility of environmental factors at the prenatal stage (Wing, 2007).

Barriers to learning and participation

The key barriers to learning and participation have been discussed above. These can be summarised as follows.

- Impairment in the ability to understand social behaviour.
- Impairment in the ability to understand and use non-verbal and verbal communication.
- Impairment in the ability to think and behave flexibly.

(TDA, 2008)

The government's strategy for SEN, *Removing Barriers to Achievement* (DfES, 2004), identifies the importance of:

- early intervention to ensure that children receive the help they need as soon as possible;
- removing barriers to learning by embedding inclusive practice and strategies to support children;
- raising expectations and achievement by developing teachers' skills, knowledge and confidence;
- delivering improvements in partnership with parents and other agencies.

As a trainee teacher or even as a qualified teacher you are not expected, nor would it be appropriate for you, to make a diagnosis of autism. However, you may have observed specific characteristics in a child which may cause you to question whether the child may have ASD. The diagnosis must *be made on the pattern of development of skills and behaviour from infancy onwards* (Wing, 2007, 25) and should, where possible, be made by a multidisciplinary team made up of health professionals. Medical professionals may consult with teachers during the process of making a diagnosis.

As a trainee teacher you will want to implement strategies to remove potential barriers to learning and to increase participation and achievement. Some strategies are suggested below. It is vital that you develop positive and respectful relationships with parents and other professionals who may be involved with the child. You should aim to implement any recommendations made by outside agencies and you should discuss the child's progress regularly with your teacher-mentor, parents or carers.

It was mentioned above that children with ASD might be sensitive to certain stimuli. Some may be sensitive to light or temperature. Others might be sensitive to specific textures such as sand, soil or certain foods. It is possible that children may display sensitivities with specific smells, such as the smell of perfume or after-shave. Teachers need to be aware of these sensitivities so that children are not placed in stressful situations. Of course, these sensitivities may become barriers to learning. How can you engage children in sand play or water play in the Early Years Foundation Stage if they have a specific sensitivity with sand or water? How can you teach a lesson relating to light if a child becomes distressed with bright lights? How can you create a colourful and stimulating classroom environment if a child is sensitive to colour or becomes distracted with displays? These are all critical questions which you may need to ask yourself, and there are no magic answers. Sometimes you may avoid putting the child in a specific situation. At other times it might be appropriate for you to gradually give the child experience of specific stimuli.

Strategies to support learning

If you have a child with autism in your class on placement, the first thing you need to do is to research into this area thoroughly. You need to talk to your teacher-mentor to find out which strategies work and identify any strategies that do not work. All children are individuals and will respond differently to interventions. Amaladoss (2006) stresses the importance of a whole-school approach. All staff, including teaching and support staff, need to have knowledge of the particular child and the strategies which are being employed to manage the child's behaviour and learning. Teachers need to meet with parents and carers to discuss their approach and to agree on systems for managing the child's behaviour. A daily home–school diary is a very useful way of communicating with parents and allows successes and challenges to be shared.

Creating safe learning environments

As a trainee teacher you need to ensure that the tasks that you are providing do not include elements of social learning which are beyond the capabilities of the child. Identify the intended learning outcomes and focus on how these are best achieved for individual pupils. Review your classroom provision and pedagogical approaches. Could they be responsible for creating undesirable behaviours? Remember the social model of disability and how it conceptualises disability as a social construct caused by factors that are external to the child. A classroom which lacks structure and routine could generate undesirable behaviours. Many children with ASD are visual learners. Capitalise on this and take account of this when you plan learning opportunities. Resources should be clearly labelled using both words and pictures. Think carefully about providing calm areas and areas that provide quiet spaces for work. Individual workstations may be appropriate for some learners with ASD but some children may be able to happily work alongside their peers. The needs of the child should determine your classroom organisation. Consider whether you need to use lighting. The flicker of fluorescent lighting may be distracting and patterns can be a source of fixation. Excessive use of colour or overcrowded displays may also be distressing.

You will need to ensure that the rest of the class are understanding and knowledgeable about children with ASD. Talk to them about the child's specific difficulties and ways in which they might be able to offer support. However, it is important not to conceptualise any form of disability as a personal tragedy. The aim is not to seek tolerance and sympathy from others, but to create an ethos where diversity is viewed positively and celebrated. The social model has helped to emancipate and empower disabled people, and teachers need to ensure that children with ASD are not viewed as inferior.

Unstructured social times such as playtimes and lunchtimes may be difficult for children with ASD. Some children with ASD may choose to walk the perimeter of the playground or follow lines on the floor to avoid social contact. Some children may run around flapping their arms because they feel distressed. All staff need to be aware of how to communicate with children with ASD. This includes lunchtime staff. Some children with ASD can gently be encouraged to join in with playground games. Initially the game will need to be modelled by an adult and you may decide that a game with one partner is sufficient. You can then judge whether it is appropriate to increase the size of the group, depending on the specific needs of each child. Some children may be happy to be left alone and should not be forced to socially interact.

Visual approaches

Adults with autism have described how pictures enable them to think (Grandin, 1996). Visual timetables provide children with a clear structure to the day and help to reduce anxiety (TDA, 2008). The daily schedule can be presented horizontally or vertically and laminated picture cards can be attached to denote the daily activities. Symbols or photographs are used to represent the tasks, activities or lessons that are to be completed during a day. The child can then access the visual timetable at the start of the day and know the sequence through which s/he will work through the tasks. Whole-class visual timetables support a more inclusive ethos and ensure that no child is singled out from the rest.

A visual timer (TDA, 2008) with an arrow will help children to see how much time is left in a lesson. Choice cards can be offered at the end of an activity and symbol cards can be used to give specific commands.

CASE STUDY

A whole-class approach to inclusion

Sally was a Reception teacher and was preparing for a child with autism to join her class. Luke was four years old. He displayed all the traits of classic autism. He had no speech and was unable to socially interact. His parents had adopted the use of a visual timetable at home and this was working well. Sally was keen to build on the strategies that Luke was already familiar with. She decided to talk to the class about autism. She explained that Luke often got very upset if he did not know what was going to happen during the day and she showed the children an example of a visual timetable. She discussed how important it was for Luke to know the order of his daily activities. Sally was surprised when several other children also expressed a desire to know what was going to happen during the day. She asked for their suggestions and the children were given some 'thinking time' to come up with suggestions.

The children decided to create a planning board. The children's names were printed on cards and displayed on the board. Cards were then created representing different classroom activities (sand, water, mathematics, literacy, construction, mark-making, computers, etc.). Each child was given a set of 12 cards representing the different activities in the classroom. These were stored in each child's tray. On a daily basis, the children were given 'planning time' where they were required to select the activities they wanted to do that particular day. Activities relating to literacy and mathematics were placed on the board daily by the teacher next to a specific time slot. However, there was flexibility about which of the remaining activities the children selected and the order in which these were undertaken. After selecting the relevant cards, these were then displayed by the child on the board next to their name in the order of their choice. At the end of the day the cards which had been displayed on the board were removed and were not available for future selection until the child had used up all their remaining cards.

REFLECTIVE TASK

- Why was this approach more inclusive?
- How did the teacher involve the pupils in the decision-making?
- Do you think it was a good move to talk to the whole class about autism?

Picture exchange communication system (PECS)

PECS is a communication system for children with no speech. In this system if a child wants an object, they must firstly search through their personal book of picture symbols to find the relevant picture that represents the sought object. The child can then offer the picture in exchange for the desired object. This strategy prevents lack of speech becoming a potential barrier to participation. After this initial stage children can then be introduced to a simple phrase such as *I want*, which they may learn to use before offering the symbol. Phrases or words can then be attached to Velcro strips in the PECS book and the adult can model the phrase by verbalising it and the child may repeat this. Initially PECS will be used in situations where the child will be motivated to communicate, such as when they require food. Its use can then gradually be extended to cover other purposes.

Structure and routine

The visual timetable described above will help to outline the daily structure. However, simple routines must be consistent and this is beneficial to all children. Try to implement consistent early-morning routines. For example, what do the children do when they first enter the classroom in a morning? Where do they put their lunch boxes? Where do you ask them to sit? What are the early-morning activities? Then think carefully about the routines during the day. How do you stop the class and gain their attention? Do you play a particular piece of music at the end of a session when the children are tidying away? Where do the children line up? Where are the resources kept? There are so many things for you to think about but try to keep changes to a minimum and if changes are necessary, these should be communicated in advance.

Social stories and comic strips

Social stories are a strategy developed by Carol Gray (Gray, 1994) in the US. Some children with ASD may find particular situations or experiences difficult. A social story is built around this experience and aims to describe the events that happen and the feelings of the characters in the story. They can help children learn to cope with specific social situations, such as going to the dentist, having their hair cut, lunchtime or going into assembly. Children can read these stories prior to an event (or have them read out) to help them rehearse the experience.

Comic strip conversations can be used as a way of representing social situations, similar to social stories. They are made up of stick people, and speech and thought bubbles so that children can think about the sequence of events, what was said during a particular situation, and the thoughts and feelings of the people involved in the experience (Amaladoss, 2006).

Individual teaching

The decision for a child to receive individual teaching is a professional decision informed by the needs of each child. You will need to discuss the teaching style with parents and carers. They may be keen to avoid too much individualised teaching and this may be the reason why they have chosen to send their child to a mainstream school in the first place. Some children with ASD may have specific needs that mean that social learning is not possible. Some children with ASD may be able to cope with some peer–peer interaction combined with some individual teaching. Some learners with ASD may not need individual input and it may be possible to support these learners in a group situation. You will need to exercise your professional judgement in the decision-making process.

Adequate staffing ratios are essential if you are supporting a child with ASD. If individual teaching is appropriate, you should make use of bookcases, cupboards and screens to create a working space for the child with ASD. However, you should be aware that such approaches could perpetuate segregation. In developing your systems for classroom organisation you should consult with specialist staff from other agencies who are involved in supporting the child. For younger children with ASD, individual workstations may be appropriate, whereas older children may be able to work at an open table (TDA, 2008). You will also need to make decisions about whether they work alone at an open table or whether they can work in parallel, opposite another child or working alongside a group of children.

Classroom environment

The flicker and hum of fluorescent lighting may cause a distraction for learners with ASD. Think carefully about possible sensitivity to light. Classroom blinds can be used to good effect to minimise light. Think about the visual appeal of your classroom. Try to avoid brightly coloured backing paper. Use calming colours instead. You could divide the classroom into low-stimulus areas and high-stimulus areas. In the low-stimulus area there could be minimal display and calming colours. This might be the most appropriate place for the child with ASD to work. However, other children could also work in this area. In the high-stimulus area there could be colourful displays of pupils' work. This solution is a compromise to balancing the needs of one child against the needs of all children (TDA, 2008).

PRACTICAL TASK PRACTICAL TASK **PRACTICAL TASK** PRACTICAL TASK **PRACTICAL TASK**

Arrange to meet a specialist teacher from the communication and interaction team in the local authority. You may get the chance to shadow one of these teachers during your placement or you may have to meet at the headquarters. Find out about their role and responsibilities. Find out how the service supports practitioners and parents or carers. Find out about how teachers are able to undertake further professional training within this field in order to become specialist teachers of autism.

ICT

Many children with ASD have visual learning styles, although some children will demonstrate other learning styles (TDA, 2008). For this reason, the computer can be a very powerful learning resource for children with ASD. Try to make the learning visual. Teachers should maximise the use of the interactive whiteboard during lessons and children with ASD should have frequent opportunities to explore a range of software. Sometimes, they may develop a preference for a specific piece of software and this can, in itself, become a barrier to learning. You should gradually aim to increase their experience of a range of software in order to give each child access to a broad and balanced curriculum. The use of a personal laptop computer with a range of software specifically targeted at learners with ASD may increase motivation in some sessions. It may be appropriate to section off the computer area with screens so that this does not cause a distraction to the child with ASD when they are working in other areas of the classroom. The use of headphones for children working on computers may minimise levels of distraction.

PRACTICAL TASK PRACTICAL TASK **PRACTICAL TASK** PRACTICAL TASK **PRACTICAL TASK**

Arrange to spend some time in a local authority resource base for children with autism or a school which includes learners with autism. Your ITT provider may arrange this for you but if not you could pursue your own professional development during your periods of 'flexible training'. This will need advance planning as the children may need to be 'prepared' for you visit. Spend some time observing in the setting.

- What visual strategies are used to support teaching and learning?
- How is the teaching space organised?
- How are the children taught?
- What behaviour management strategies are adopted?
- How are the staff deployed to support teaching and learning?

Talk to the lead teacher and discuss the following points.

- What are the specific needs of learners with ASD?
- What strategies are used to support teaching and learning and why are these strategies used?
- How do staff in the setting work in partnership with external agencies and parents or carers?

Managing anger

If you have a child in your class with ASD you are advised to keep a mood diary. The purpose of a mood diary is to look for triggers that may cause a child to become angry or distressed. If you are able to identify the trigger you may be able to reduce the expressions of anger. Some children may benefit from being taught to sit in a calm place until the feelings of anger have subsided. Remember to reward the child when s/he stays calm. Ensure that you consistently model positive values in your teaching – an angry teacher could produce angry children.

CASE STUDY

Attitudes to inclusion

Read the following episode, written by a parent of a child with autism.

His teacher had very low tolerance levels. He would shout at Sam all the time and Sam used to cry constantly. He used to send him out of class with his TA when he couldn't cope with him. Sam became a very distressed little boy. I am sure that he just knew that Mr X didn't like him. Mr X just doesn't recognise that children are not all the same and cannot be programmed to behave in the same ways. Children are not robots. I saw all my hard work going down the drain and it made me so angry. I found out one day Sam was wailing and screaming because Mr X had shouted at him. I couldn't believe what Mr X did. He tape-recorded him and took it round the staff and played it to them. He wanted to humiliate Sam. I was furious and so was the SENCO (Bev) because she told me what had happened. Bev was deeply disturbed by the tape and she told Mr X that it said more about him and his classroom ethos than it did about Sam. Mr X clearly thought the tape was funny and was laughing about it in the staffroom. I was appalled.

REFLECTIVE TASK

- What do you think the parent means when she says that *children are not all the same and cannot be programmed to behave in the same ways*?
- What do you think the parent means when she says *I saw all my hard work going down the drain*?
- How important are teachers' attitudes in fostering an inclusive ethos?
- Why do you think Mr X demonstrated such unprofessional behaviour?

CASE STUDY
Managing individual needs

Michael was placed in a Year 2 class within a mainstream school. Initially there were occasions when Michael demonstrated signs of distress. He cried and screamed and the other children quickly became frightened of Michael and were reluctant to go near him. The teacher decided to keep a behaviour diary. She recorded the events leading up to an incident and she later analysed the episodes with Michael's support worker. Upon analysis it was evident that Michael's 'outbursts' occurred when there were sudden changes to his routine. He had a visual timetable but changes to routines were frequent and not uncommon in primary schools.

Working in partnership with Michael's parents, a policy was established to help Michael cope with sudden changes to his routine. A staff meeting was called and in the meeting it was agreed that any changes to routines had to be communicated to Michael's support worker first. This strategy enabled the support worker to pre-warn Michael of changes to his routine. The support worker was then able to explain what was about to happen, using either a social story or a visual comic strip. This approach was very successful and Michael soon learnt to cope with changes to his routine. On one occasion Michael even took part in a fire drill without getting upset, because he had already been prepared before the event took place.

REFLECTIVE TASK

- How useful was the behaviour diary?
- Do you think a behaviour diary would be useful for parents?
- Why did Michael get upset?
- How was the issue addressed?

CASE STUDY
One size fits all?

Read the following extract from a teacher who had a child with ASD in her class.

The advisory teacher from the local authority seemed to have 'textbook' strategies for dealing with children with autism. She insisted that David had a daily schedule, even though I thought that we should try him without one in the first instance. I was anxious not to make him feel different. She said that he had to be escorted to the toilet. She wanted him to go out to play before the others so that he was not distressed by being in a busy cloakroom. She said that David would need one-to-one support on the playground. She wasn't very happy because I said 'no' to all of her recommendations. These strategies would have isolated David and were not practical in a mainstream classroom and a mainstream school. There was simply no way that we could escort him everywhere and the bottom line was that his parents had chosen to send him to a mainstream school for a reason. They did not want us to operate a mini special school. She also wanted David to have one-to-one teaching, which I am totally opposed to. I was glad when she left us alone. After a couple of days he settled brilliantly. He didn't need a schedule. He didn't need one-to-one supervision and he didn't need to be taught in a one-to-one situation. He coped with getting ready to play with the other children. He coped with our normal classroom routines. Sometimes I remember that he used to throw himself on the floor. This was often when he needed his own space. We used to withdraw him to give him the space he needed but not as a punishment. It allowed him to calm down.

REFLECTIVE TASK

Think carefully about the following questions.

- Why was the teacher reluctant to implement the suggested strategies?
- Do you think the teacher was right to avoid implementing the suggested strategies?
- How might the adoption of special school practices in mainstream environments perpetuate exclusion rather than inclusion?
- What do you think are the dangers associated with labelling?

A SUMMARY OF **KEY POINTS**

> **Children with Asperger syndrome may have average or above-average IQ levels and well-developed speech, but essentially children in both groups typically share commonalities.**

> **Children with ASD typically display impairments in the three areas of social interaction, social communication and rigidity of thought and behaviour.**

> **Visual systems, such as visual timetables and PECS, can be used to support the specific needs of children with ASD.**

MOVING *ON* > > > > > > **MOVING** *ON* > > > > > > **MOVING** *ON*

Now that you have developed a basic understanding of the specific needs of learners with ASD, try to arrange a short placement in either a school for learners with autism or in resourced-based provision attached to a mainstream school. Find out about the systems that are used to organise the teaching and find out about strategies which staff use to manage challenging behaviour.

REFERENCES REFERENCES **REFERENCES** REFERENCES **REFERENCES** REFERENCES

Amaladoss, K. (2006) 'Supporting children with autistic spectrum disorders in a mainstream classroom', in G. Knowles (ed) *Supporting Inclusive Practice*, 111–125. London: David Fulton.

Bailey, A., LeCouteur, A., Gottesman, I., Bolton, P., Simonoff, E., Yusda, E. and Rutter, M. (1995) 'Autism/Asperger syndrome: a strongly genetic disorder: evidence from a twin study', *Psychological Medicine*, 25, 63–77.

DfES (2004) *Removing Barriers to Achievement: the Government's strategy for SEN*. Nottingham: DfES.

Grandin, T. (1996) *Thinking in Pictures: And Other Reports from My Life with Autism*. London: Vintage.

Gray, C. (1994), *The Social Storybook*. Arlington, TX: Future Horizons.

Jordan, R. and Powell, S. (1995) *Understanding and Teaching Children with Autism*. Chichester: John Wiley and Sons.

Jordan, R. (2005) 'Autistic spectrum disorders', in A. Lewis and B. Norwich (eds) *Special Teaching for Special Children,* 110–122. Berkshire: Open University Press.

Kanner, L. (1943) 'Autistic disturbances of affective contact', *Nervous Child,* 2, 217–250.

Kanner, L. and Eisenberg, L. (1956), 'Early infantile autism, 1943–1955', *American Journal of Orthopsychiatry*, 26, 55–65.

Rutter, M. (1999) 'Autism: Two-way interplay between research and clinical work', *Journal of Child Psychology and Psychiatry*, 40, 169–188.

TDA (2008) *Special Educational Needs and/or Disabilities: A training resource for initial teacher training providers: primary undergraduate courses.* TDA.

Warnock, M. (2005) *Special Educational Needs: A New Look,* Impact No.11, Philosophy of Education Society of Great Britain.

Wing, L. (2007) 'Children with Autistic Spectrum Disorders', in R. Cigman (ed) *Included or Excluded: The challenge of the mainstream for some SEN children.* Oxford: Routledge.

Wing, L. and Gould, J. (1974) 'Severe impairments of social interaction and associated abnormalities in children. Epidemiology and classification', *Journal of Autism and Childhood Schizophrenia*, 9, 11–29.

FURTHER READING FURTHER READING FURTHER READING FURTHER READING

The following texts provide excellent reading material to help you understand autism.

Haddon, M (2003) *The Curious Incident of the Dog in the Night-time*. Doubleday.
Sainsbury, C. (2000) *Martian in the Playground*. SAGE.

Useful website

www.autism.org.uk/autism This website by the National Autistic Society has a wealth of background information about autism.

7
Supporting children with behavioural, emotional and social difficulties

Chapter objectives

By the end of this chapter you should:

- **understand the complexities of social, emotional and behavioural difficulties;**
- **understand how these complexities affect teaching and learning;**
- **be able to implement some strategies in order to support these children;**
- **be aware of the support from outside agencies.**

This chapter addresses the following Professional Standards for the award of QTS:

Q2, Q10, Q18, Q19, Q21a, Q21b, Q31

Links to: Every Child Matters, SEN Code of Practice.

Introduction

Children do not come to school as 'empty vessels'. Irrespective of their background all children are shaped by their social environment, and while for most this has a positive impact on their learning within school, for some it can sadly be a barrier.

It is often argued that social, emotional and behavioural problems have their roots in 'nurture' rather than 'nature', but irrespective of the cause you as a teacher have to support these pupils while maximising their educational potential.

Emotional difficulties

Short term – minor: minimal effect, e.g. goldfish dying.
Long term – major: far-reaching effects, e.g. family crisis.

A child's emotional state can severely affect their learning and while the actual emotion may be relatively easy to pinpoint, e.g. tears, withdrawal, etc., the causes are not. Children often find emotion very difficult to deal with, as do many adults, and may actually be scared of their strength of feelings. It is often a belief that emotion is not something to be shared and that we should assume a 'stiff upper lip' – further contributing to existing problems.

Social difficulties

As a person you have your own norms and values and possibly a strong ethos of what you consider right and wrong. However, as a teacher you will come into contact with many things that radically challenge these beliefs, and it is imperative that these in no way cloud your judgement when involved with a child with social problems. What is considered the norm in some families may raise cause for concern from other parties, but this does not necessarily indicate that a child's problems are as a direct result of what some may perceive as 'unusual' circumstances.

Maslow's *Hierarchy of needs* (1954) concluded that all human behaviour has a meaning and is a response to a drive to have needs met. The first and baseline need in this hierarchy is 'physiological or survival needs', these being the basic needs of food, warmth and shelter. However, it is an unfortunate fact that not all pupils you come into contact with will have these needs met on a regular basis, and as such will find it very difficult to move to the next level of need.

The next level, safety needs, can again be a challenge for some pupils as they do not always experience environments that make them feel physically and emotionally secure.

The third level, 'love, affection and belonging', is another aspect that can be lacking in pupils' lives and which can severely affect the next level, which is 'self-esteem'.

The final level, 'self-actualisation', is when we can be motivated to realise our potential, an aspect we strive for all our pupils but which can be difficult to achieve due to previous needs not being met.

At every level some chidlren may feel challenged and possibly powerless to change their circumstances and it can often be this aspect which can manifest itself in challenging behaviour. As teachers we need to be aware of the possible lack of basic needs and address these to the best of our ability within an educational setting, e.g. breakfast clubs, creating secure environments and working areas, giving positive and supportive feedback, and giving all children the chance to be creative and autonomous.

However, on a final note, do remember that we all have limitations and that you can only be expected to do your best.

Behavioural difficulties

Children do not come to school trained in how to behave properly.

(Wright, D., 2005).

How many times have you heard a child referred to as 'naughty'? Yet, when you have had time to get to know them you begin to realise there is more to it than a 'naughty' streak.

Behaviour manifests itself in many ways and can severely disrupt the learning of the child concerned and their classmates. It can be as a result of social and emotional problems or of an underlying special educational need.

Whatever the cause, the behaviour has a function for that child, and this will be discussed later in the chapter.

REFLECTIVE TASK

Have your encountered children on your placements who you now believe to have underlying problems which could have begun to explain their behaviour? How difficult was it to identify these problems? Were you able to access records which gave an insight into possible causes of their behaviour?

School policies

Schools should have a clear vision for managing behaviour through establishing clear rules and boundaries, with emphasis on the positive. In formulating a policy in the primary school, it is most important to ensure that there is an agreed message, philosophy and understanding of which everybody is aware, in order to achieve a consistent and coherent approach throughout the school.

(Shelton and Brownhill, 2008)

Within your placement schools you will have the opportunity to view policies relating to many aspects of school organisation and curriculum. The behaviour policy may be a stand-alone document which encompasses all aspects, e.g. the school's policy on sanctions and rewards, or there may be several policies relating to different aspects. It is well worth asking to see these policies in order that you can familiarise yourself with the school's arrangements prior to classroom experience.

Medical implications

For some children behaviour difficulties can be linked to medical problems and in some cases the medication that is used to treat it. These problems can be both physical, e.g. epilepsy, or mental, e.g. depression, and in these cases the intervention and support of medical professionals are vital.

Data collection by type of SEN (DfES, 2005) cited by Pomerantz *et al.* (2007) states:

Pupils with a range of difficulties, including emotional disorders such as depression and eating disorders; conduct disorders such as oppositional defiance disorder (ODD); hyperkinetic disorders including attention deficit disorder (ADD) or attention deficit hyperactivity disorder (ADHD); and syndromes such as Tourette's should be recorded as behavioural, emotional, or social difficulties (BESD) if additional or different educational arrangements are being made to support them.

Behaviour that is medically based can be difficult to modify. However, it is still in the child's best interest to instigate whatever measures possible in order that the effects of the behaviour are minimised and the child is given the opportunity to achieve their potential.

Behaviour management or behaviour modification?

It goes without saying that teaching a child with behavioural difficulties can be very hard work. It often involves extra planning, making changes in the physical environment, and liaising with others, to name but a few, and time can play a big part in this.

While behaviour management can be time consuming, it is usually considered that behaviour modification is more so, and so poses even further demands on the teacher. However, the rewards of modification are usually more positive and so become more beneficial in the long term.

When we talk about managing behaviour we usually mean just that – within the confines of school an individual's behaviour is managed through agreed strategies, sometimes involving physical intervention, exclusion from the group and modified tasks and activities. While this method can often minimise disruption and allow teaching and learning to continue, it does not attempt to investigate the underlying causes and so seek a solution.

As mentioned previously, all behaviour has a function – in simple terms this means that the behaviour is fulfilling some need or function for the child in question. Unfortunately the child themselves doesn't always recognise this.

Functional analysis

This involves the participation of as many individuals as possible who are involved with the child, e.g. parents/carers, medical professionals, social workers, etc. This group consider aspects of the child's life that are both positive and negative, and through shared and open discussion begin to link behaviours to life experiences. This can often be a long and in some cases a painful experience for those involved, but can give a starting point for modifying behaviour. A case study best illustrates this method.

CASE STUDY
Changes for Simon

Although Simon was often quiet and withdrawn in school his behaviour gave no cause for concern. He found it difficult to concentrate and ongoing assessment identified possible learning difficulties. However, successive teachers were very positive about Simon as he was making progress. When Simon entered Year 6 his behaviour changed dramatically: he was loud and abusive and would often attempt to hurt classmates for no apparent reason. Exclusion from the group, differentiated tasks and 'time out' had little or no effect and the problem was escalating.

A group meeting was called but his parents were very reticent about attending, although they agreed to do so following reassurance from the school. All seemed to be very positive in Simon's life and it was becoming increasingly difficult to explain his behaviour. It was decided to reconvene the meeting at a later date.

In the interim period his parents contacted the school, wishing to share information and were invited to speak to the headteacher as they felt unable to share with a larger group. They were obviously upset and the father explained that as an 11-year-old boy he had transferred to secondary education (the school where Simon was to go) where he was bullied to the extent that he felt it was still affecting his life. He had never shared this with anyone or received help, and hadn't realised that Simon had overheard arguments when aspects had been discussed.

It therefore seemed apparent that to Simon, Year 6 signalled the fast-approaching transfer to a school of which the only knowledge he had was inadvertently from his dad. It was felt that he was unable to share this with anyone as he felt a loyalty to his dad, and his mechanism for coping was his inappropriate behaviour.

Subsequently, Simon was able to undertake many very positive visits to the school, some even with his dad, and as a result he became much more confident and self-assured about the transfer. The behaviour he displayed also began to diminish, and at the point of transfer showed none of his previous problems.

Also on a positive note his dad received support in order to resolve his own problems.

This was a very positive outcome and one that was arrived at relatively easily. This however is not always the case, as the 'answer' to the behaviour problem can be very difficult and sometimes impossible to source. However, whenever possible this method is extremely beneficial, and one which ultimately will enhance your teaching.

Attention deficit hyperactivity disorder

Approximately 5% of school age children have ADHD. This means that there will be, on average, one or two children with ADHD in every single classroom.

(O'Regan, 2002)

The Attention deficit hyperactivity disorder (ADHD) diagnosis should not be applied to a child who appears 'naughty' or displays behavioural difficulties. In most cases the children who do have ADHD genuinely do not set out to be disruptive or defiant and are often distressed by their own behaviour.

A multidisciplinary approach needs to be adopted with these children as professionals such as speech and language therapists and doctors can be hugely beneficial in supporting these pupils both at home and at school.

The ABC model

This method is also beneficial in ascertaining why a pupil may be behaving in a certain way, and so offers a way forward with a solution.

- **A** Antecedents – What is the context of the behaviour?
- **B** Behaviour – What is the behaviour?
- **C** Consequences – What happens afterwards?

Antecedents

What was the task – Why might the pupil find this challenging?

What environment is the pupil working in – can this cause a challenge? For example, some children find confined spaces a problem.

Who is the child working with – both staff and peers? Is there any recorded incidents involving these individuals?

Are the work/resources presented differentiated appropriately in order that the child can achieve?

What happened immediately before the behaviour? Was there a trigger? Did the child come into school from home in an anxious state?

Behaviour

What exactly is the behaviour that is causing concern? Is there more than one type of behaviour? Are all behaviours linked or could they have different triggers?

What are the reactions displayed by the child? Are these reactions observed in other contexts?

Consequences

What happens when the behaviour ends? Does it actually end or does another behaviour take its place?

Does the child appreciate that there has been a change in their own behaviour? Do they have the opportunity to discuss this with anyone?

Do they have an understanding of why they display such behaviour?

What reactions do they get from adults and peers? Does this reaction actually help or does it inflame the situation, e.g. peers who make fun of actions or behaviour? Consider that some other children might actually find the behaviour of others as a positive aspect – it may take the attention of the teacher from them or distract the class from having to complete their work.

What happens next? But most importantly, what as a teacher do you do next?

The ABC model needs to be more than a paper exercise that is completed after the event. It needs to be used as a tool to build an accurate picture of behaviour, in order that a solution can be sought. As with functional analysis, this is not always an easy or straightforward process, but it is worth the time invested in it if a solution towards supporting a pupil can be found.

PRACTICAL TASK PRACTICAL TASK **PRACTICAL TASK** PRACTICAL TASK **PRACTICAL TASK**

Consider a pupil with behaviour difficulties you have had experience of on your placement. Use the ABC method to analysis their behaviour. Talk to other staff who have worked with the pupil – do they agree with your findings?

Behaviour of teacher

You can be irritable during a lesson and Susan will raise her eyebrows and keep a low profile. Charlotte will believe your irritation is personally directed at her and will quickly start creating difficulties.

(Howarth and Fisher, 2005)

It is often stated that children learn by example, and as such a teacher can be a very influential role model. It therefore goes without saying that a teacher should be a positive influence, especially when dealing with children with social, emotional and behavioural problems.

The language that a teacher uses can have a significant effect on pupils, sometimes resulting in them being labelled. Negative language does not support or enhance self-esteem, and by only slightly modifying what we say we can turn a negative into a positive.

Social and emotional difficulties

While social and emotional problems can have a significant impact on both a child's ability to learn and their behaviour, it is an aspect that is often best addressed by other professionals. This does not, however, negate your responsibility to a child with social and emotional problems, and it is imperative that you are able to support these children by understanding the role of others.

You may have already encountered children on your placements that for whatever reason are negatively affected by their social circumstances and or their emotional state, and no matter how strongly this affects you, in common with many other teachers, you can feel that your 'hands are tied'.

Therefore on any placement you must be made aware of the school's child protection officer/teacher, their role within school, and the school procedure for reporting incidents including those of a social and or emotional nature.

This designated person will, if necessary, be able to alert other professionals, e.g. social workers, medical personnel, to the case and deal with it in an appropriate manner.

However, it is still the class teacher who will ultimately have to deal with the child on a day-to-day basis, and as mentioned earlier a non-judgemental approach needs to be taken. Children with social/emotional problems often lack structure and boundaries to their life and by creating these in the classroom the child can feel more secure and so able to learn. These children will also often confide in you as a trusted person in their life, and once again it is vital that you are aware on the school's policy for reporting disclosures.

Schools are well aware that pupils need a very broad curriculum in order to enhance their social and emotional skills, and as a teacher these can become an integral and enjoyable part of everyday teaching.

PRACTICAL TASK PRACTICAL TASK **PRACTICAL TASK** PRACTICAL TASK **PRACTICAL TASK**

On your next placement note the professionals and outside agencies who work with pupils in school. If possible investigate their roles and how their input impacts on pupils.

Emotional state of teacher

It should never be overlooked that teachers are actually human and as such can be affected by the same problems as some of our pupils. In fact for some teachers, the problems being encountered by a pupil can be significantly disturbing if they themselves have also had personal experience of this. Although often very difficult to do, it is in your own best interest to alert someone within the school if you are having difficulties, who can either guide and support you, or refer you to someone who can. This is not a weakness on your part, it is in fact a strength as you need to be emotionally fit if you are to be able to help and support your pupils.

Professional relationships

Within *Every Child Matters: Change for Children* (DfES, 2004) there are five key outcomes. These are:

- be healthy;
- stay safe;
- enjoy and achieve;
- make a positive contribution;
- achieve economic well-being.

It is intended that each child achieves these outcomes through the support and guidance of a multidisciplinary approach, involving a range of professionals, including teachers and others who work in school settings.

For children with social, emotional and behavioural problems the notion of 'joined-up working' is even more imperative, and it is very often the teacher who will identify and instigate this.

However, there is not always the positive outcome we desire from this way of working. Wilson and Pirrie (2000) cite Clark (1993), who states:

> It is clear from the literature that putting people together in groups representing many disciplines does not necessarily guarantee the development of a shared understanding.

Working with parents and carers

> Research has shown a clear association between behaviour and conduct problems in early childhood and parenting practice that is characterised by harsh and inconsistent discipline, low levels of positive parental involvement and poor monitoring and supervision.
>
> (DfES, 2003)

In an ideal world, teachers, along with other professionals, would have the full co-operation and support from parents and carers in all aspects of the child's life. However, we know that this is not always the case, and it is unfortunate that due to many factors, the parents and carers of children with social, emotional and behavioural difficulties cannot always offer this support.

Some parents/carers may be affected in a similar way to their children by, for example, emotional difficulties, while some may not appreciate or may not want to appreciate the problems.

Teachers, along with other professionals, often find the support of parents/carers invaluable in all aspects of a child's development and they should be included at every level. For example, a behaviour modification plan which is carried out consistently at home as it is in school is usually far more effective than one which is school based only.

However, we must be realistic and concede that for whatever reason we may not have parental involvement or co-operation, and that while this may cause even further difficulties, it must not impede the support that we and other professionals can give to the child.

> *It is our experience that parents typically tend to feel (in their encounters with school staff) that they are somehow being blamed for their child's misdemeanours.*

(Gray, 2002)

Planning for pupils with social, emotional and behavioural difficulties

Trainees will be well aware of the QTS standard which expects them to *Plan for progression across the age and ability range for which they are trained, designing effective learning sequences within lessons and across series of lessons and demonstrating secure subject/ curriculum knowledge.*

You will also, no doubt, have a fast-growing awareness of the need for effective differentiation of lessons in order to meet the needs of all learners. However, planning for children with social, emotional and behavioural difficulties can often add a new dimension to both the planning and the delivery of a lesson. In some circumstances it is not what a child learns but how, and this is especially true of this group of children. With this in mind it may not be the content of the lesson which needs differentiating, but the method of delivery coupled with the child's preferred learning style.

As mentioned previously, children often lack boundaries and structure to their lives, and sometimes all that is needed are these elements in order to enhance teaching and learning. Some examples of how this can be put into practice are as follows.

- Clear outcomes for all lessons in a form understandable to the pupil.
- Clear timetables, once again in an understandable form that is adhered to.
- Now and next.
- Resources clearly labelled and accessible.
- A secure working environment.
- Rewards and sanctions.
- Rules and routines.

Clear outcomes

Ensure that the child actually knows what they are going to learn and what is expected of them. This can be presented in words, pictures or symbols. The child may also require continual reassurance throughout the lesson that they are following the correct 'learning path'.

Clear timetables

A clear overview of the day – again in a variety of formats. For some children a certain subject or area of school can be challenging. A clear overview gives time for the child to adapt and prepare for the transition.

Now and next

For some children the overview of the day is too complex or challenging, although they still require the security of what is to come. 'Now and next' gives them exactly what it says – what is expected of them immediately and what will happen next. Ensure that all aspects of the day are recorded on this e.g. playtimes, snack time, etc., as well as lesson times. Once again this can be in a variety of formats. In some cases children may require a three-part 'plan' – what they have just achieved, what they are working on, and the next step. It will be your professional judgement which ascertains the degree of security you need to build into a pupil's visual timetable.

Resources

Ensure that children understand where resources are stored and how to access them. For some children opening a drawer marked 'pencils' and finding nothing but rulers could in itself be the trigger for negative behaviour. Clear labels using words, pictures, symbols or even the 'real thing' are vital, and a child's self-esteem can be given a positive boost if they are able to be responsible for the retrieval and collection of resources.

Secure working environment

It goes without saying that we all hope to create a classroom or working area that is secure. However, for some children this security may not be enough and they will require a modified area in which to work. Some children actually need to create their own area in which to work – a personalised desk or an enclosed space, and giving them this will hopefully lead them in time to becoming fully inclusive within the classroom space. Security can also often be achieved through a well-organised and tidy environment, an aspect which is not always a part of their life out of school.

REFLECTIVE TASK

Think about the classrooms and working areas in your placement schools. Have they been conducive to safe and secure working? What small measures could have been put in place to enhance these aspects?

Rewards and sanctions

One of the most contentious issues in the management of children with behaviour problems is the use of rewards and sanctions. There still appears to be a strong belief that children with challenging behaviour need discipline through sanctions as that 'will learn them'. Rewards should be for good behaviour and performance it is true, but in reality rewards also affect long term change in behaviour while sanctions in practice only hold the behaviour in check for a short time.

(O'Regan, 2006)

The majority of pupils we teach respond positively to rewards, and while we do not want to get into a culture of 'bribery', they can be a very effective motivator. In contrast, sanctions need not be negative and can even be designed to complement rewards.

Pupils often respond more positively if they have the opportunity to choose their own rewards and this can often include other learning opportunities, e.g. time on the computer.

When building rewards into the curriculum it is important that you consider the time element, i.e. how long will the reward last until the pupil is expected to move to another activity? For pupils who find telling the time problematic, timers are ideal, especially if you want to aim to extend the time on task and reduce the reward time. Now and next cards can include rewards, and for some pupils the 'next' will often need to be a reward. A reward or star chart is often all that is needed in order to motivate, and while a class chart is beneficial for those who achieve, for those that find competition challenging a personalised chart will be more acceptable.

Sanctions need to be understood by the pupil if they are to be effective, and an off-the-cuff *sit there for five minutes* will do little good if the pupil does not understand why. As with rewards, sanctions need to have a time implication which the pupil understands, and as previously mentioned can have a positive implication, e.g. you can still have your chosen reward but due to your behaviour you now need to have five minutes out before that can happen.

Pupils with behavioural difficulties often require almost 'instant' rewards and sanctions, and working towards a reward to be given on Friday when it is only Monday will have little or no effect.

As with all aspects of teaching and learning, a reward or sanction system can be differentiated to be effective for all class members and in doing so will create a greater feeling of inclusion for all pupils.

Rules and routines

Classroom rules should be positive rather than negative. They should indicate what to do rather than what not to do, and should reflect desired behaviours and positive ways of working.

Teaching and learning styles

Again, referring to the standards, you are aware that you are required to *use a range of teaching strategies* and *know how to personalise learning.* This of course refers to all pupils you will teach, but this aspect may have greater relevance for those with social, emotional and behavioural problems.

- Visual learners – these learners need to see the teacher's body language and facial expression (difficult for pupils on the Autistic spectrum). They may think in pictures and learn best from visual displays.
- Auditory learners – learn by talking things through and listening to what others have to say. Written information may have little meaning until it is heard.
- Kinaesthetic learners – learn through moving, doing and touching. They need to actively explore the world around them. They find it hard to sit for long periods and can become distracted by their need to explore.

CASE STUDY
Lack of instructions causes problems for Neil
Neil was a 14-year-old boy with behavioural difficulties. He attended a mainstream school and had the support of a teaching assistant for two hours each day. His attainment levels were below those of his peers.

I observed him during a geography lesson and was seated in the classroom when he arrived in the room. His teaching assistant was also in the room but had been asked by the teacher to prepare resources and was busy doing so when he arrived. He arrived calmly and took his seat. There was a quite high noise level with other pupils coming in from play and it seemed that the teacher expected them to go to their places and complete the various worksheets that had been handed out without any introduction or input. Neil sat for at least ten minutes and remained calm, he was not on task, his teaching assistant was still otherwise engaged and he seemed interested in his peers who were eventually settling and beginning to work. After ten minutes it became apparent from his body language that he was becoming agitated and he suddenly leapt from his chair, ran to the fire exit, kicked it open, and ran across the school grounds. I was informed later than he was found up a tree. The teacher informed me that he often displayed this type of behaviour and that someone would eventually find him and return him to class.

You have probably come to the conclusion as I did, that he found the whole situation very stressful and that the only course of action was to escape. He had been denied his allocated support; he found the noise level difficult, and he was aware that his peers were able to access and complete the allotted work while he was not.

When I was able to speak to him however, his major concern was the format of the work he was expected to complete and the lack of structured instructions. He said he needed someone to tell or show him what do even though he was capable of reading instructions, and that he needed pictures of diagrams in order to understand the task. Needless to say the worksheets consisted solely of text. He also said that he was happier completing practical tasks, but that he never got the opportunity.

A change in teaching style for this pupil would have been extremely beneficial, and while it was not the only barrier to his learning it was certainly significant. The pupil has now transferred to a special school and is responding extremely well to a curriculum and learning styles better suited to his needs.

A SUMMARY OF **KEY POINTS**

> It could be argued that even the 'experts' don't fully understand the complexities of all social, emotional and behavioural problems and their causes. However, during your career take each case as it is presented, and remember you can only do your best.

> Use the opportunities presented by these pupils to enhance your teaching, for the benefit of all pupils you will encounter over the years.

> Understand that there is a wealth of expertise to be gained from colleagues, literature and research. Use this wisely – you won't have time to reinvent the wheel when working with pupils with difficulties.

> Be aware of, and develop relationships with, other professionals. Keep the ethos of Every Child Matters in the forefront of your mind. Asking for help is not a weakness – it is a strength that will ultimately benefit the pupils you teach.

MOVING *ON* > > > > > > MOVING *ON* > > > > > > MOVING *ON*

Many trainees preparing for their placements often view pupils with social, emotional and behavioural difficulties with trepidation. However, it can be these very pupils who enhance your placement by challenging your teaching and giving you valuable experiences which will enhance your professional development for many years to come. It must also be remembered that you will not be the first teacher to have to deal with a specific problem, and that there is a wealth of expertise, support and resources available in order to help you teach these young people successfully, usually with very rewarding outcomes.

FURTHER READING FURTHER READING **FURTHER READING** FURTHER READING

Adams, K. (2009) *Behaviour for Learning in the Primary School*. Exeter: Learning Matters.

Cohen, L., Manion, L. and Morrison, K. (2006) *A guide to teaching practice*. Abingdon: Routledge.

Farrell, M. (2008) *Educating Special Children – An introduction to provision for pupils with disabilities and disorders*. London: David Fulton.

Roffey, S. (2006) *Helping with Behaviour*. London: Routledge.

REFERENCES REFERENCES **REFERENCES** REFERENCES **REFERENCES** REFERENCES

DfES (2003) *Every Child Matters*. London: DfES.

DfES (2004) *Every Child Matters: Change for Children*. London: DfES.

Gray, P. (ed) (2002) *Working with Emotions – Responding to the challenge of difficult pupil behaviour in schools*. London: Routledge.

Howarth, R. and Fisher, P. (2005) *Emotional and Behavioural Difficulties*. London: Continuum.

Maslow, A. (1954) *Motivation and Personality*. London: Harper and Row.

O'Regan, F. (2002) *How to teach and manage children with ADHD*. Wisbech: LDA.

O'Regan, F. (2006) *Can't Learn, Won't Learn, Don't Care – Troubleshooting challenging behaviour*. London: Continuum.

Pomerantz, K., Hughes, M. and Thompson, D. (eds) (2007) *How to Reach 'Hard to Reach' Children – Improving access, participation and outcomes*. Chichester: Wiley.

Shelton, F. and Brownhill, S. (2008) *Effective Behaviour Management in the Primary Classroom*. Maidenhead: OU Press.

Wilson, V. and Pirie, A. (2000) 'Multidisciplinary team working indicators of good practice', Spotlight 77, *The Scottish Council for Research in Education*, 1–4.

Wright, D. (2005) *There's no need to shout! – The Primary Teacher's Guide to Successful Behaviour Management*. Cheltenham: Nelson Thornes.

Useful websites

www.teachernet.gov.uk
www.tda.gov.uk
www.nasen.org.uk
www.goodschoolsguide.co.uk/sen
www.behaviour4learning.ac.uk
www.everychildmatters.gov.uk

PART 3

THE WIDER CONTEXT

8

Developing partnerships with pupils and parents

Chapter objectives

By the end of this chapter you should be able to:

- **understand the expectation that pupils with SEN have a right to participate in all decision-making processes relating to their education;**
- **understand your duty to communicate effectively with parents or carers in all decision-making processes relating to children with special educational needs;**
- **consider ways in which you might facilitate effective partnerships with pupils and parents.**

This chapter will address the following Professional Standards for the award of QTS:
Q1, Q3a, Q4, Q5, Q6

Introduction

This chapter considers the importance of schools providing pupils and parents with a voice in decision-making processes. This is especially important in relation to the education of children with special educational needs. Traditionally, pupils and parents were excluded from decision-making processes in education. In fact, it is not that many years ago that parents were often kept at arm's length from schools and teachers. Professional knowledge was privileged and held in high esteem. However, current educational policy stresses the importance of schools working in partnership with pupils, parents and other agencies. The notion of education as a partnership may present some schools and teachers with interesting challenges. Effective practitioners will need to reflect on their own values and judgements in relation to effective partnership working. In order to meet the requirements of the current policy agenda, all agencies including parents and children must have a voice. This chapter will provide examples of how barriers to pupil and parent voice have been overcome. Throughout this chapter we have made several references to Early Years principles and practices from the Early Years Foundation Stage (EYFS) framework (DfES, 2007). These principles and practices should be embedded in high-quality Early Years settings. These principles and practices should continue to be evident throughout Key Stages 1 and 2 and underpin high-quality inclusive practice.

REFLECTIVE TASK

REFLECTIVE TASK

As a trainee teacher you already have an extensive knowledge and understanding of curriculum frameworks, teaching strategies and assessment for learning. Consider how additional input from children with special educational needs and their parents or carers could enhance your knowledge and further support the child. Think carefully about the following questions.

- What are your personal feelings and views about parent partnership and pupil voice?
- Do you think pupils and parents can make a valuable contribution to education?
- Do you think it is right that pupils and parents should influence pedagogy?
- Consider the advantages to this wider partnership.
- Consider the challenges and how they might be overcome.

Partnerships with pupils

The Code of Practice for Special Educational Needs (DfES, 2001, 27) stresses the *right of children with special educational needs to be involved in making decisions and exercising choices*. This highlights the importance of parents, carers and practitioners working in collaboration with the child. This duty thus ensures that children with SEN are able to express their views, needs and feelings regarding matters that affect them. They are entitled to a voice.

Parents and practitioners should carefully reflect on how they might develop effective partnerships with children with SEN. They may consider all or some of the following ways of including the viewpoints of children in decision-making process.

- The setting of learning targets and contributing to IEPs.
- Discussions about choice of schools.
- Contributing to the assessment of their needs and to the annual review and transition processes.

(DfES, 2001, 27)

The importance of empowering all children to express their views and opinions is embedded within the *Every Child Matters* agenda. All children, including those with special educational needs, will develop higher self-esteem if their needs, feelings and views are discussed and acted upon. Practitioners and parents have a responsibility to create opportunities for children to communicate their thoughts and feelings. However, simply listening is not enough. Where possible and appropriate, the child's voice must be considered and acted upon.

However, a word of caution is offered in relation to the notion of child voice. Children have varying levels of experience, maturity, skills and knowledge and some children may need appropriate support in helping them to express their needs, views and feelings. You will need to consider carefully the ways in which children with little or no verbal communication skills can be effectively included in such a process.

REFLECTIVE TASK
REFLECTIVE TASK

In relation to such a challenge you need to consider the following.

- What are the potential barriers to seeking children's perspectives?
- How might these barriers be overcome?

CASE STUDY

Giving every child a voice

Read the following case study and think carefully about how the practitioner overcame the difficulties of seeking the child's voice in the decision-making process.

Talik was six years old when he moved schools. He entered his new setting with a statement but records were incomplete. Talik had no language and avoided social interaction. The diagnosis indicated that Talik had autistic spectrum disorder. Talik found changes in routine extremely difficult. At the point of his entry to his new school his parents had recently separated and he had also moved house. As a result of this Talik joined his new setting in a distressed state and it was vital that meaningful routines were established as quickly as possible.

The school had contact with both Talik's mother and father, although he lived with his mother. In an attempt to identify Talik's interests, a transition meeting was held with Talik's previous school. He was observed in this setting. The new school met with Talik's mother and had a separate meeting with his father. During these meetings Talik's interests were discussed. However, the practitioner was aware that his new setting could offer additional interests for Talik. It was therefore important that Talik could express his own view. The practitioner was aware of the challenges associated with Talik's inability to communicate his views verbally and this potential barrier had to be overcome.

Feelings cards (a smiley and a sad face) were introduced to Talik. Initially the practitioners used these to convey their own feelings to Talik. When he did something that pleased them they showed the smiley face and said *I am happy.* If Talik demonstrated inappropriate behaviour the sad face was shown as the practitioner said *I am sad.* After several days the same two cards were given to Talik. He was working on a computer, which the practitioners knew he enjoyed. In this situation the practitioner trialled the use of the cards to determine Talik's ability to use them appropriately. Talik was asked *Is Talik happy or sad?* The practitioner pointed to the appropriate card to reinforce the symbol that represented each feeling. Talik responded by selecting the smiley face and he handed it to the practitioner.

Over several weeks Talik was introduced to a breadth of new experiences and he was asked to indicate his view and feelings by using the happy and sad symbols. This enabled the practitioners to identify Talik's likes and dislikes. Practitioners in the setting were then able to use Talik's interests as a vehicle for teaching and learning.

REFLECTIVE TASK

- What were the barriers to giving Talik a voice in his own learning?
- Can you think of other strategies that could have been implemented to effectively address these barriers?

REFLECTIVE TASK

Having considered this case study, consider ways in which you might use visual systems to support children with communication, speech and language difficulties in making effective contributions to discussions relating to their needs.

It is important that all children, including children with SEN, have the opportunity to contribute and participate in all aspects of school life. For example, many schools now operate a school council system, which elicits the views and opinions of children in relation to many aspects of school life. It is essential that children with SEN also be provided opportunities to be representatives on such councils. There may be perceived barriers to their participation but these should be considered, addressed and overcome. For some learners with communication difficulties, it may be appropriate for a third party to convey their views.

Some parents or professionals may be reluctant to seek the perspectives of children. Well-meaning parents and practitioners may feel that they are better informed to make decisions for the child. Seeking a child's views and opinions can unearth unexpected information that should be considered in decision-making processes. The Code of Practice emphasises that *children and young people with special educational needs have a unique knowledge of their own needs and circumstances and their own views about what sort of help they would like to help them make the most of their education* (DfES, 2001, 27).

From a very young age all children should be encouraged to express their opinions and feel that these should be valued. The EYFS framework advocates the need for children to make choices and decisions in their learning and this helps them to feel secure, confident and valued. Children with special educational needs must never be an exception to this principle and you must take steps to facilitate this expectation. You should ensure that children with special educational needs are able to make contributions to their own IEPs and their learning targets. They should also be involved in monitoring and reviewing their own progress, thus empowering them with a sense of achievement.

CASE STUDY
Pupil participation and evidencing achievement

Suzie entered a Reception class at the age of four years and ten months. She had no language and had poor social skills. Her mother had chosen for her to be educated in a mainstream setting.

One of her IEP targets was to develop her social interaction with known adults and other children, as Suzie consistently preferred to play alone and well away from the proximity of other children. Over a period of several months Suzie's tolerance to other people encroaching on her personal space began to improve. Several strategies were planned and implemented to facilitate social interaction. Initially a known adult would sit a short distance away from Suzie, ensuring that they were engaged in a different activity. Once she was able to tolerate this invasion of her personal space the adult began to offer comments relating to the activity that Suzie was engaged in. Suzie gradually began to acknowledge the presence of the adult by giving them eye contact when they spoke to her. The next step was to offer support, often in the form of additional resources, to enhance Suzie's play. At this point Suzie became confident to work in close proximity alongside the known adult. After this, a known child was introduced into Suzie's personal space. Observations indicated that the additional child unwittingly invaded Suzie's space more than the adult had done. Suzie tolerated this invasion of her personal space and the practitioners subsequently introduced additional children so that Suzie was working alongside a small group of children. The practitioners in the setting noticed that Suzie no longer identified areas where she could play in isolation. She chose to work in areas of the classroom that she enjoyed and the presence of other children in these areas was no longer an issue.

The teacher was anxious to evidence this development and a video diary was kept to document Suzie's progress. Suzie was present at her own annual review and, as anticipated, stayed closely by her mother's side and made no eye contact with the unknown adults in the meeting. The video diary was presented to evidence the progress that Suzie had made and everyone valued the opportunity to see first-hand Suzie's achievements. Most of all Suzie clearly enjoyed the video diary and pointed at herself throughout.

REFLECTIVE TASK

How did the school facilitate pupil participation in this review meeting?

Consider other ways in which you could have given Suzie a voice. Discuss this with one of your peers.

One or more agencies may be involved in supporting a child with special educational needs. It is vital that all those involved in supporting and assessing children seek the views of the child. The child's views should be included in formal reports of progress. Teachers should create regular opportunities to collect children's perspectives of their progress and achievements. You should therefore ensure that the child's voice is included in learning journals or assessment records. There is an expectation that the views of all stakeholders should be valued and included in the child's records of achievement.

Case Study

Negotiating contracts with pupils

Tommy was eight years old and had already been placed in four schools. He had been excluded on one occasion due to his disruptive behaviour. This had a detrimental impact on the education of his peers. It was commonplace for Tommy to physically and verbally assault his peers and members of staff. He frequently crawled under tables, ran around the room hitting children over the head and on one occasion he blocked the exit to the classroom so that children could not leave. He physically assaulted the headteacher and was verbally abusive to a member of support staff.

Tommy was working at School Action Plus. The educational psychologist suggested that Tommy be given ownership of his own targets for development. As with all children it is important to acknowledge their strengths, and Tommy was no exception. With this in mind Tommy was invited to an informal discussion with his class teacher. It was deemed important that the conversation began in a positive manner and the teacher had collected a range of Tommy's work that was worthy of praise. This work was discussed with Tommy. In addition the teacher focused on times when Tommy had displayed positive characteristics including kindness, caring and general consideration for others. Tommy responded positively to this one-to-one interaction and the positive nature of the discussion. Tommy was then invited to elaborate further on other things he did well.

Following this Tommy was asked to consider five targets for his own development. He immediately focused on his behaviour and he was given the opportunity to reflect upon what he did and the impact on other children. Interestingly the discussion highlighted a number of triggers including the fact that he found speaking and listening sessions difficult, the sessions were too long and he hated filling in worksheets. The practitioner acknowledged Tommy's views and suggested that together they formulated plans and drew up an agreement that both parties would adhere to. It was agreed that Tommy would concentrate and aim to participate in speaking and listening sessions for ten minutes. After this time he was allowed to access his 'choose box', a box created by Tommy containing things of personal interest. After the first week there were two successful days followed by one day when Tommy had 'broken' the agreement. The practitioner reminded Tommy that they had an agreement and that he had not adhered to it. Over a period of several weeks there were some inconsistencies in his behaviour but generally Tommy was noticeably less disruptive. Worksheets were replaced by practical tasks and observational assessment was used to track Tommy's progress.

REFLECTIVE TASK

- How did the practitioner empower Tommy?
- How could other children have perceived this situation and how might you address this?

PRACTICAL TASK PRACTICAL TASK PRACTICAL TASK PRACTICAL TASK PRACTICAL TASK

During your placements you may well encounter children who appear to lack interest and motivation. Identify these children; consider patterns in their behaviour and responses and possible triggers. Reflect upon the positive attributes of each child and ensure that you convey these to them. Encourage them to identify their own strengths and areas for improvement.

Partnerships with parents

The Code of Practice for Special Educational Needs (DfES, 2001) and the *Every Child Matters* agenda strongly promote the need for schools to develop effective partnerships with parents of children with special educational needs. Before reading this section it is useful for you to consider your own values in terms of developing partnerships with parents or carers.

REFLECTIVE TASK

REFLECTIVE TASK

- Do you value parental contributions?
- Do you think parents should be able to influence practice in schools?
- Do you believe that parents hold vital information about their child that would be useful for you to access?

A vital consideration when formulating partnerships with parents or carers is that parents are a child's first teacher. The Early Years Foundation Stage framework (DfES, 2007) states that:

> *Parents are children's first and most enduring educators. When parents and practitioners work together in early years settings, the results have a positive impact on children's development and learning.*
>
> (DfES, 2007, 2.2)

Children never develop at a faster rate, both physically and mentally, than during their formative years. Much of this time will have been spent with parents or carers. Parents and carers hold key information regarding children's strengths, interests and anxieties. This information enables practitioners to build an early and accurate picture of a child. Parents and carers may have ideas and opinions and these must be taken into consideration. Most parents will have their child's best interests at heart and an effective partnership between parents and schools is an essential means through which to best support and develop a child.

Teachers may have a wealth of professional experience with which to support and develop a child. However, it is vital that this does not dominate and overrule the opinions of the parents and carers. Parents of children with special educational needs may be anxious about their child's progress. They need to be reassured that teachers are working with them in the best interests of their child. It is vital that parents feel that their concerns are taken seriously and that teachers are doing their very best to enable their child to reach his/her full potential.

The value of strong parent–school partnerships will ensure that targets for a child's development are formulated and reviewed collaboratively. However, the strongest partnerships will ensure that this effective practice is embedded and reinforced by daily communication between home and school. This can effectively be addressed through the use of daily home–school diaries. Practitioners and parents or carers should use these diaries to communicate the child's strengths and thus communicate the child's achievements. Communication which overemphasises what the child cannot do may damage partnerships between home and school. This is pertinent in the case of a child with behavioural issues. Parents and carers do not need a daily diary entry regarding their child's challenging behaviour. They are already aware of this and are working with you to address relevant targets. As a trainee teacher you should therefore focus on identifying positive aspects of a child's development. There is of course a need to record the child's 'next steps' but these should be Small, Measurable, Achievable, Realistic and Timed (SMART targets).

Think carefully about the way in which you communicate with parents. You will need to think about the clarity of your diary entries. It is important to avoid jargon, which some parents may not understand. You also need to communicate 'negatives' with extra care and attention. It is important to provide parents and carers with advice on how they can support their child to achieve the targets that have been set. Think about how you will communicate with parents who do not speak English. This may present a considerable challenge. You may need additional support to address this. Some parents may be reluctant to work with you in partnership. They may be influenced by their own negative experiences of school and some parents may not value education. Additionally some parents may have problems in their own personal lives, which they may not wish to share with you. This can impact negatively on the school–parent partnership. These are real challenges facing professionals in school. Schools can encourage parent partnership but there is no obligation for parents to comply. Ultimately, whatever resistance you are faced with, you must do your best to meet the needs of all children. Your efforts to develop effective partnerships with parents and carers must be consistent and ongoing, even in the face of adversity. Practitioners must have high expectations for every child and with or without the support of parents they must endeavour to raise outcomes for all.

Teachers/practitioners should ensure that they consult with parents or carers when making decisions about the appropriate level of intervention (graduated response) for their child. Practitioners should ensure that parents fully understand the graduated response and their role within the Code of Practice. Parents or carers should be involved at all stages of the graduated response and they should be consulted and advised about specific interventions that will be implemented to support the child. Parents or carers should be fully involved in monitoring and evaluating the success of interventions and the setting of new targets.

Parent Partnership Services

The Parent Partnership Service (PPS) is available to all parents and is provided through the local authority. It is the duty of the local authority to ensure that parents have access to and understand information, advice and guidance. The PPS provides independent parental support for parents of children with special educational needs. It can provide them with clear information regarding rights, roles and responsibilities. In addition the service can support parents in contacting additional services that may be able to support them and their child.

Schools should inform parents about the PPS and ways in which it can help them. The service is inclusive of all parents and carers and information is available in a variety of formats and languages. In addition the PPS offers training to teachers and governors relating to working more effectively with parents. The service offers an independent parental supporter for all parents. This facility ensures that parents and carers are able to access neutral and reliable information regarding their rights.

Parents may be keen to fight for the rights of their child. This creates a 'them and us' situation. If effective, respectful and supportive relationships are established with parents then a team ethos can be created where everyone can work together for the benefit of the child. Effective partnerships are based on mutual respect. All parties within the team need to feel that they are working together towards a common aim. In the best partnerships practitioners and parents are able to listen to each other and be honest about their own strengths and opinions, while working in a non-judgemental manner.

CASE STUDY
Valuing the parent voice

Stephen was in his first term of his Reception class. He displayed a range of inappropriate behaviours. On a daily basis he physically assaulted staff and pupils and he refused to follow the routines and expectations of the classroom. His personal, social and emotional development was well below age-related expectations. His skills in all other areas of learning were also below age-related expectations.

The class teacher invited Stephen's mother into school to discuss her concerns. Initially the teacher needed to establish whether Stephen was aggressive at home as well as at school. His mother confirmed that this was the case and she provided possible explanations for his behaviour. These included the fact that Stephen rarely saw his father. His father was a member of the Armed Forces and he was in active service. The teacher made a note of the information provided by Stephen's mother.

Stephen's mother was almost relieved that his behaviours had been noted in school, as she had, until this point, felt that Stephen reacted only to her in this way. She thought that she was quite simply a poor parent. The teacher suggested that Stephen be placed on School Action and that she would work closely with Stephen's mother. Together they identified five focused targets that Stephen needed to achieve. Through discussion Stephen's mother and the teacher identified the ways in which these targets could be addressed both at home and in school.

A consistent approach from both parties was deemed essential in terms of the management of Stephen's behaviour. It was agreed that a home–school diary should be introduced to ensure open and regular communication between both parties. It was also felt that Stephen's mother needed moral support and the teacher suggested that she should have a short meeting with her at the end of each week to discuss progress against the targets. Stephen's mother welcomed this suggestion. In this way it was possible to review progress frequently, and together Stephen's mother and the teacher were able to set new targets.

After half a term Stephen's behaviour had improved both at home and at school. This gave Stephen's mother more confidence. There was now a strong parent–school relationship and over time Stephen's mother became more open in her communications with the teacher. She sought advice but notably had the confidence to offer advice too.

REFLECTIVE TASK

How did the teacher demonstrate that she valued the voice of the parent?

How did the teacher minimise any power differentials?

Consider other ways in which you might have empowered Stephen's mother in this process.

Stephen's mother was eager to work in partnership with the school to support her son. What would you have done if Stephen's mother had been a reluctant participant in this process?

PRACTICAL TASK PRACTICAL TASK **PRACTICAL TASK** PRACTICAL TASK **PRACTICAL TASK**

Consider establishing manageable systems while undertaking your placements, which would ensure that children's achievements at home can be conveyed to the teacher and celebrated in the classroom.

PRACTICAL TASK PRACTICAL TASK **PRACTICAL TASK** PRACTICAL TASK **PRACTICAL TASK**

Now consider establishing manageable systems while undertaking your placements, which would ensure that children's achievements in school can be conveyed to parents or carers and celebrated at home.

Perspectives of parents

Barbara Cole's research (Cole, 2005) with mother-teachers found that parents' experiences of raising a child with SEN influenced their professional thinking. The study found that these teachers developed greater empathy when working with parents of children with SEN after raising their own child. The mother-teachers became more conscious of the feelings of the parents. This research illustrates that personal experiences can impact on professional practice. These professionals became more acutely aware of the impact of their use of language on the parents. They became aware of how abrupt and 'clinical' they may have previously been when talking to parents.

Cole's research has implications for all teachers who work with children with SEN. Think carefully about what you say to parents and your tone of voice. Many parents of children with SEN may have experienced emotional challenges and will already be aware that their child finds some aspects of life challenging. Others may not be aware that their child is encountering any difficulties. You need to be sensitive in the way you communicate your concerns to the parent. It is crucial that you do not overemphasise 'within-child' factors and that no blame is apportioned to either the child or the parent. You must keep an open mind. The child's difficulties could have arisen due to inappropriate 'teaching' either at home or school. The child's difficulties could well be biological, but appropriate teaching could help to minimise these. It is essential that you listen carefully to the parents' perspectives, concerns and opinions. It must be a two-way conversation and both parties must be fully included in the discussion. Joint problem-solving is essential. The Early Years Foundation Stage framework states that:

> *Effective communication means there is a two-way flow of information, knowledge and expertise between parents and practitioners...Parents and practitioners have a lot to learn from each other. This can help them to support and extend children's learning and development.*

> (DfES, 2007, 2.2)

The teachers in Cole's study wanted their own children to be treated with dignity and care and this impacted on their professional practice. From this study it is evident that parents value the progress their child makes but they give equal value to the child's holistic needs. Reflect on your own attitudes towards children with SEN. Do you treat them all with care, dignity and respect? Consider the way you communicate with these children and their parents or carers. Ensure that you are sensitive to their needs and feelings. Aim to develop their self-esteem and confidence.

Cole found that the mother-teachers often valued words of encouragement and *an arm around the shoulder* (Cole, 2005, 338). An open-door policy would clearly facilitate regular and meaningful communication between teachers and parents. It is not necessarily the amount of time offered to a parent that proves to be the most productive element of good communication. The key element is the ability to display genuine interest in a child and its parents. The little things really do matter. These may include the following points.

- Giving parents time when they need it.
- Ensuring that there are opportunities for sharing incidental information.
- Providing opportunities for parents to celebrate their child's achievements as well as sharing their concerns.
- Sharing mutual successes and challenges.
- Developing an honest and open professional relationship.
- Developing an atmosphere of mutual respect.

Cole found that the mother-teachers needed to feel, above all else, that schools and teachers genuinely wanted and welcomed their child (Cole, 2005). This has vital and far-reaching implications for all teachers. The initial meeting with all parents and their child is one of the, if not the most important, points of contact. Parents may be understandably judgemental at this stage. They are ready to embark on trusting you with the education and care of their child. This is a huge responsibility and privilege and you must understand the huge importance of your role. Always ensure that you:

- smile;
- listen;
- interact positively with the child;
- ask questions to create a better picture of the child's needs, interests and strengths;
- answer questions about your systems and routines, ensuring that the parent and child are also able to develop a clear picture of you and the school;
- assure parents that your systems are flexible to accommodate the specific needs of their child;
- invite the parent and child to visit the working classroom;
- introduce the parent and child to other practitioners in both the classroom and the wider school;
- provide opportunities for the child to interact with their peers and adults.

Consider how the visual environment of the school and the classrooms reflects diversity. A child with additional needs will feel empowered and have a sense of belonging when displays and teaching materials reflect and celebrate difference and diversity. In turn, parents or carers will greatly value a school that totally embraces diversity through:

- positive attitudes towards all children and an atmosphere of mutual respect between all members of the school community;
- displays that celebrate diversity;
- teaching materials that reflect diversity;
- adaptations to meet the needs of all learners.

> ## CASE STUDY
>
> A parent has approached the teacher on several occasions and is becoming very intolerant of her daughter's behaviour. The mother frequently needs to express her frustrations to the teacher in relation to her daughter. The teacher is able to relate to many of the concerns raised by the mother. The child has been placed on School Action and targets to support the child have been jointly agreed between the school and the mother. However, it is apparent that the mother expects the school to fully address the situation. The mother is not fulfilling her role in supporting her daughter in meeting the targets on the IEP. The mother explains that she works and has two other children and quite simply does not have time to devote to supporting her daughter in terms of her behaviour.

REFLECTIVE TASK

Discuss with your peers the ways in which you would encourage a reluctant parent to work in collaboration with you to support their child's development.

Parents as partners

Clough and Nutbrown (2004) found that although there was broad agreement that parents should be involved in the early education of their child, there were some reservations from pre-school practitioners in relation to parent partnerships. One practitioner expressed concerns regarding parental involvement in formal meetings. The concerns raised were that parents often found it painful to hear of and accept their child's misdemeanours (Clough and Nutbrown, 2004). A small minority of participants in the research highlighted the potential difficulties faced by some parents in supporting the needs of their child due to their own problems (Clough and Nutbrown, 2004).

There are several implications arising from this research. Professional should think carefully about how they frame the child within formal meetings. Emphasis should be placed on acknowledging and celebrating the child's strengths. The starting point for any meeting between professionals and parents should focus heavily on what the child knows and can do. In meeting with parents and carers it is important to think carefully about the following points.

- The strengths of the child: acknowledge progress and avoid unnecessary comparisons with national norms.
- How you intend to demonstrate that you genuinely care about the child.
- How you intend to convey that the child belongs and is welcome in the school and the classroom.
- Communicating your desire to help the child. Never apportion blame.
- Valuing parental perspectives and contributions.

As professionals we must acknowledge that parents of children with SEN may also have their own specific needs, although it is important not to stereotype. An atmosphere of mutual respect and trust must be created in order to give parents the confidence to share their own difficulties. Some parents may have specific difficulties with aspects of literacy or numeracy and these issues may prevent them from supporting their child. An inclusive ethos must not solely focus on children. In an inclusive school all children, staff, parents and carers should work in collaboration in a non-judgemental atmosphere. It may be helpful and advantageous to advise parents and carers about adult learning opportunities, which they may wish to access. These may be available within the school or local community. Inclusive schools will operate an open-door policy, so that parents are able to gain first-hand experience of their child's education. This will deepen the parents' and carers' knowledge and understanding of teaching and learning, and facilitate consistency in the use of approaches. The Early Years Foundation Stage framework states that:

> *Parents can be helped to understand more about learning and teaching through workshops on important areas such as play, outdoor learning or early reading. Some parents may go on to access further education at their own level.*
>
> (DfES, 2007, 2.2)

These strategies can help parents to overcome their own barriers to learning, thus empowering them to be able to support their child's education.

Diverse family structures

There may be some significant challenges in terms of establishing positive parent partnerships, which you need to be aware of. It is important that you are proactive in establishing partnerships with all parents. However, in the context of working with children with SEN, parent partnerships are critical, as they will ultimately help to raise pupils' levels of achievement.

During your placements you will experience and meet a wide range of families. The make-up of these families will vary. Never assume that all children live with both parents. Some children reside with only one of their parents. Others may live with carers or other relatives. Some children may live with same-sex parents. Additionally a different language may be spoken at home. You may be educating children of refugees, asylum seekers or travellers. It is important that you value and respect all families and that they are all offered the same opportunities to contribute to and support their child's education. All barriers should be identified and removed.

Professional development to support you in working with all families is essential. Anti-discriminatory and anti-bias practice is important. Your classroom displays should reflect a range of home languages. You may need to think about planning specific events to engage fathers in education. You should actively seek the perspectives of all families. Communication to parents needs to be accessible and with some parents you may need to communicate through an interpreter or through the use of sign language. An inclusive ethos means that all parents and carers are provided with opportunities to express their views and can expect to have them acted upon. Practitioners cannot possibly have the skills to address every eventuality. Inclusion is an ongoing process, not a product. It would not be unusual to encounter several challenges during your career. Each challenge needs to be met with determination and *good faith and effort* (Cole, 2005). You cannot be expected to have all the tools in the teaching toolbox. You are expected to acquire tools as and when you need them during your career.

RESEARCH SUMMARY RESEARCH SUMMARY **RESEARCH SUMMARY** RESEARCH SUMMARY

Desforges, C. and Abbouchaar, A. (2003) *The Impact of Parental Involvement, Parental Support and Family Education on Pupil Achievement and Adjustment: A Review of Literature,* Brief No: 433. Nottingham: DfES.

This research identifies a positive correlation between parental involvement and pupil achievement. The research found that levels of parental involvement are influenced by social class and children's attainment. In addition the research found that levels of parental involvement tend to diminish as children get older.

A SUMMARY OF **KEY POINTS**

> **This chapter has considered the importance of providing pupils, parents, carers, practitioners and teachers with an equal voice.**

> **All parties have valuable contributions to make and by working together they will create strong building blocks for effective partnerships.**

> **Pupils and parents should be involved in all decision-making processes and they should be treated as equal partners in the learning process.**

MOVING *ON* > > > > > > MOVING *ON* > > > > > > MOVING *ON*

Now that you are aware of the importance of developing partnerships with pupils and parents you should consider speaking to parents of children with special educational needs about their vision of an inclusive education for their child. You could ask them for suggestions on ways in which you could develop your practice. This will create a genuine opportunity for providing parents with a voice. Try to take account of their recommendations in your practice.

REFERENCES REFERENCES **REFERENCES** REFERENCES **REFERENCES** REFERENCES

Clough, P. and Nutbrown, C. (2004) 'Special educational needs and inclusion: multiple perspectives of preschool educators in the UK', *Journal of Early Childhood Research,* 2 (2), 191–211.

Cole, B.A. (2005) '"Good faith and effort?' Perspectives on educational inclusion', *Disability and Society,* 20 (3), 331–344.

Desforges, C. and Abbouchaar, A. (2003) *The Impact of Parental Involvement, Parental Support and Family Education on Pupil Achievement and Adjustment: A Review of Literature,* Brief No: 433. Nottingham: DfES.

DfES (2001) *Special Educational Needs Code of Practice.* Nottinghamshire: DFES.

DfES (2007) *The Early Years Foundation Stage: Setting the standards for learning, development and care for children from birth to five.* Nottingham: DFES.

FURTHER READING FURTHER READING **FURTHER READING** FURTHER READING

The Early Years Foundation Stage framework is accompanied by a CD-ROM resource, which has a wealth of literature related to parent partnership. There are also some interesting case studies that exemplify successful parent partnership in practice.

The SEN Toolkit, which accompanies the Code of Practice for SEN, provides useful guidance on developing pupil and parent partnerships.

Useful website

www.standards.dfes.gov.uk/parentalinvolvement/ This website provides case studies which show examples of how schools have increased parental involvement.

9
Developing partnerships with outside agencies

Chapter objectives

By the end of this chapter you should:

- **be aware of the outside agencies most likely to be involved with pupils, and understand their roles and responsibilities;**
- **understand the principles of collaboration with outside agencies within the *Every Child Matters* framework;**
- **know where to seek further assistance when involved with pupils with special educational needs.**

This chapter addresses the following Professional Standards for the award of QTS:

Q3a, Q6, Q20, Q33

Links to: *Every Child Matters*, SEN Code of Practice.

Introduction

The *Every Child Matters: change for children* policy (DfES, 2004), which resulted in the Children Act (2004), set out to address, and eradicate, the problems of agencies not working in collaboration, which resulted in the unfortunate and possibly preventable death of Victoria Climbié. It is even more unfortunate that cases such as these are still making the news, but it will only be by every professional being involved with children working in true collaboration that these cases will be no more.

As a teacher your roles will be many, but you need to be aware of other professionals who are available to help and support the children you teach, in order to give every pupil the opportunity to achieve the five outcomes to:

- be healthy;
- stay safe;
- enjoy and achieve;
- make a positive contribution;
- achieve economic well-being.

REFLECTIVE TASK

Choose two children from your placements who have very differing abilities. Could you have evidenced that the five outcomes were being achieved by these pupils? Was there a difference between the two? What do you think was the reason for this?

> *Meeting the special educational needs of individual children requires flexible working on the part of statutory agencies. They need to communicate and agree policies and protocols that ensure there is a 'seamless' service. Working supportively and in partnership with parents and the children and young people themselves will ensure that everyone involved understands the responses of the professionals concerned, and lead to a better quality of provision.*
>
> (SEN Code of Practice, DfES, 2001)

This chapter will endeavour to give you an awareness of the principal agencies you will encounter and liaise with as a teacher. It will highlight their main roles and responsibilities and suggest how their input can be beneficial to the children you teach.

The list of agencies in this chapter will not be exhaustive, nor is it definitive, and by contrast there may be agencies highlighted that you will never need or encounter. However, it is in the best interests of the children you teach that you work as collaboratively as possible with other professionals to avoid any child in your care being put at risk.

Outside agencies

- Barnardos
- Behaviour support services
- Child and adolescent mental health service (CAMHS)
- Educational psychologists
- Educational welfare officers (EWO)
- Local authority support services
- National Health Service (NHS)
- NSPCC
- Occupational therapists (OT)
- Physiotherapists
- Police and youth offending teams (YOTs)
- Services for the visually impaired
- Social workers
- Speech and language therapists (SALT)
- Sure Start

REFLECTIVE TASK

Have you encountered any outside agencies on your placements? What was their role within school? Was the class teacher able to liaise with them?

National Service Framework

What is a National Service Framework?

It sets out clear standards that health, social care and other service providers have to meet.

The importance of the National Framework for Children, Young People and Maternity Services

The National Framework is the government's ten-year plan to improve services for children and young people. It aims to address the imbalance of the quality of care services across the UK and ensure that all children, young people and their families receive high-quality services which fully meet their needs. It is part of the wider programme of the Every Child Matters agenda, and applies to everyone involved in delivering services for children and young people. It is not voluntary although service providers have until 2014 to meet the agreed standards.

National Service Framework for Children and Young People

Standard descriptors and themes

1 Promoting health and well-being, identifying needs and intervening early.
- Child health programme to reduce health inequalities.
- Multi-agency health promotion.
- Healthy lifestyles promoted.
- Universal and targeted health promotion.
- Access to targeted services.
- Early intervention and assessing needs.

2 Supporting parenting.
- Universal, targeted and specialist services to support mothers and fathers.
- Up-to-date information and education for parents.
- Support for parents of pre-school children to help children develop secure attachments and to develop.
- Support for parents of school-aged children to involve them in their child's learning and behaviour management.
- Early, multi-agency support for parents with specific needs, i.e. mental health problems, addiction to drugs, alcohol, parents of disabled children, teenage parents.
- Co-ordinated service across child and adult services.
- Multidisciplinary support to meet the needs of adoptive parents/adults caring for looked-after children.

3 Child, young person and family centre services.
- Appropriate information to children, young people and their parents.
- Listening and responding to them in relation to their care and treatment.
- Services respectful to the wishes of children and young people, with improved access to services.
- Robust multi-agency planning and commissioning arrangements, i.e. children's trusts, common assessment framework.
- Quality and safety of care in delivering child-centred services.
- Common core of skills, knowledge and competencies for staff working with children and young people, across all agencies.

4 Growing up into adulthood.
- Confidentiality and consent for young people.
- Health promotion to meet needs, i.e. reduce teenage pregnancy, smoking, substance misuse, suicide, sexually transmitted infections.
- Support achievement of full potential, e.g. Connexions and youth services.

- Improved access to services and advice for those who are disabled, in special circumstances or who live in rural areas.
- Transition to full adult services.
- Additional support available for looked-after children leaving care and other young people in special circumstances.

5 Safeguarding and promoting the welfare of children and young people.

- All agencies prioritise safeguarding and promoting the welfare of children.
- Local authority children and young people's plan.
- Clarification of agencies' roles and responsibilities.
- Profile of local population to identify and assess vulnerable children.
- High-quality integrated services to meet needs of children at risk of harm, being abused or neglected.
- Effective supervision for staff working with children to ensure clear, accurate, comprehensive, up-to-date records are kept and high-quality services delivered.

6 Children and young people who are ill.

- Comprehensive, integrated, timely local services.
- Professionals support children, young people and their families in self-care.
- Access to advice and services in a range of settings.
- Trained, competent professionals providing consistent advice to assist and treat a child who is ill.
- High-quality treatment and high-quality care for those with long-term conditions.
- Prevention, assessment and treatment of pain management improved.
- Integrated children's community teams and community children's nursing services working outside hospital.

7 Children and young people in hospital.

- Care integrated and co-ordinated around their needs.
- Play for children in hospital is essential.
- Children, young people and their families treated with respect, involved in decision-making about their care, and given choices.
- Planned discharge from hospital for children.
- Hospital stay kept to a minimum.
- High-quality evidence-based care provided.
- Hospitals meet responsibilities to safeguard and promote welfare of children.
- Care is provided in an appropriate location and in a safe environment.

8 Disabled children and young people and those with complex health needs.

- Services promote social inclusion.
- Increased access to hospital and primary health care services, therapy and equipment services, and social services.
- Early identification of health conditions, impairments and physical barriers to inclusion through integrated diagnosis and assessment process.
- Early intervention and support to parents.
- Palliative care is available where needed.
- Services have robust systems to safeguard disabled children and young people.
- Multi-agency transition planning occurs to support adulthood.

9 Mental health and psychological well-being of children and young people.

- Professional support for children's mental health is available in the early years.
- Staff working with children and young people contribute to early intervention and mental health promotion

and develop good partnerships with children.
- Improved access to CAMHS with high-quality multidisciplinary CAMHS teams working in a range of settings.
- Gaps in service addressed, particularly for those with learning disabilities.
- Care networks developed and care in appropriate and safe settings.

10 Medicines for children and young people.
- Safe medication practice.
- Use of unlicensed and off-label medicines comply with local and safety standards.
- Enhanced decision support for prescribers.
- Improved access to medicines.
- Clear, understandable, up-to-date information provided on medicines to users and parents.
- Greater support for those taking medication at home, in care and in education settings – safe storage, supply and administration of medicines.
- Equitable access to medicines and to safeguard children in special circumstances, disabled children and those with mental health disorders.
- Pharmacists' expertise is fully utilised.

The aim of the above standards, which are developed to meet the needs of all children, irrespective of background or circumstances, can be applied to all pupils you teach. It is, however, Standard 8 – *Disabled children and young people and those with complex health needs* that specifically relate to pupils with special educational needs. It is these themes that will in some respect decide the partnerships that will need to be forged, but it in no way precludes the fact that a pupil with special educational needs will also need to access outside agencies in response to many other standards which relate to a pupil's well-being.

An example of the outside agencies that could contribute to a child's overall needs being met (Standard 8)
- Promoting social inclusion – social worker, EWO.
- Access to health, therapy and social services – NHS, CAMHS, OT, SALT, physiotherapist.
- Early identification – LA support services, VI teacher, HI teacher.
- Support to parents – Sure Start.
- Palliative care – NHS (hospital and community).
- Safeguarding – NSPCC, police.
- Transition planning – LA support services.

This example is not exhaustive, nor can it represent the needs of every child. It does, however, give you an insight into the partnerships that may need to occur in order to meet the needs of one hypothetical pupil that you may find in your care.

PRACTICAL TASK PRACTICAL TASK **PRACTICAL TASK** PRACTICAL TASK **PRACTICAL TASK**

Can you find evidence of the themes relating to the standards in school policies relating to multi-disciplinary working?

Roles and responsibilities of outside agencies

Barnardos

Every Barnardos project is different but each believes in the potential in every child and young person, no matter who they are, what they have done or what they have been through.'

(Barnardos, 2009)

This charity works directly with over 100,000 children, young people and their families every year, running projects in many areas, including children in care, advocacy, disability and inclusion, parenting support and young carers. It also offers training to groups and individuals such as teachers and those involved in the education of children and young people.

You may therefore come into contact with Barnardos, either through their involvement with a pupil or in their training capacity.

Behaviour support services

A behaviour support service is part of a Local Authority and works in partnership with schools, within a framework of inclusion, to help them promote positive behaviour, and to provide effective support to pupils, parents and schools where behaviour is a concern and may have an effect on achievement.

(DCSF, 2009)

The provisions within this service are decided by each local authority, but usually offer preventative services and direct support for pupils with behavioural difficulties. They are staffed by specialist teachers, e.g. for ASD pupils, and work closely with other services such as pupil referral and educational welfare.

Most pupils are supported within their existing school, but local authorities have a responsibility to provide for pupils with behaviour difficulties who have to educated other than in school. This usually takes the form of a pupil referral unit (PRU), where the emphasis is getting the pupil back into mainstream education as quickly as possible after specialist intervention.

CASE STUDY
Getting specialist support
A newly qualified teacher in a Reception class was finding it difficult to meet the needs of a particular child with specific behaviour problems. After meeting with the school's SENCO, it was decided to deploy the services of the educational psychologist. As a result of this input, it was agreed that the child was on the autistic spectrum and that specialist support needed to be accessed. The behaviour support service had a dedicated teacher for ASD pupils, who began working with the pupil and was able to give the teacher resources and strategies, in order for her to meet the needs of the pupil. Eventually the specialist teacher was able to withdraw, leaving the teacher with the strategies required.

Child and adolescent mental health services

This service promotes the mental health and psychological well-being of children and young people, and provides multidisciplinary mental health services to all children and young people with mental health problems and disorders. It ensures effective assessment, treatment and support for the young people and their families.

It refers to all services which contribute to the mental health care of children and young people, which encompasses specialist services, e.g. within the NHS, and universal services, e.g. schools, and acknowledges that this care is not only the responsibility of specialist services.

CAMHS delivers services in a four-tier strategic framework. It is intended that most children and young people will be seen at tiers 1 and 2, but it is accepted that not all children will fall neatly into a tier. It is not intended that children move up through tiers but that access to all is available as and when needed.

- Tier 1   Provided by non-specialist practitioners, e.g. health visitors, teachers and social workers. General advice for less severe problems in early development with opportunity to refer to more specialist services if required.
- Tier 2   Specialists working in community and primary care settings, e.g. psychologists, counsellors. Offer consultation, outreach and specialist intervention for children and young people with severe or complex needs. These specialists are also available to train practioners in tier 1.
- Tier 3   A multidisciplinary team working in a mental health clinic or child psychiatry outpatient department, which could include psychiatrists, psychologists, psychotherapists and occupational therapists. This service is for children and young people with persistent disorders.
- Tier 4   For children and young people with the most serious problems found in highly specialised units, e.g. eating disorder units, units for abused children – as both in- and out-patients.

It is the intention of CAMHS that there should be full participation and ownership of the process by health services, social services and education, and with this in mind, you may find that not only do you collaborate with CAMHS in your career, you also become an integral part of the team.

Educational psychologists

Educational psychologists usually form part of the local authority support team, and are concerned with children and young people who are experiencing problems in an educational setting, with the aim of enhancing their learning potential.

They work with and alongside teachers and support staff, often assessing individual pupils by means of observation, and one-to-one working (sometimes involving test materials). They will devise programmes and intervention strategies after consultation with class staff, which they can monitor on subsequent visits. They are involved in the formal recommendations which can support the statementing process, and advise both parents and educational professionals at each stage.

You may encounter educational psychologists in your classroom after referral from parents or other agencies, as well as those made by you through the schools SENCO/INCO (special educational needs co-ordinator/inclusion co-ordinator). It is quite usual for an educational psychologist to work with a large number of pupils across many educational settings, and as such you may find that time to liaise with them is in short supply.

Educational welfare officers

Under education law, parents are responsible for ensuring that their registered children of compulsory school age (5 to 16) attend school regularly. LAs have a duty to ensure that parents undertake this responsibility. The Education Welfare Service (EWS) acts on behalf of the LA in enforcing a parent's duty to provide an appropriate education.

(Teachernet, 2009)

Educational welfare officers (EWOs) aim to resolve attendance issues and support children, young people and their families when pupils are experiencing difficulties in school, or where welfare issues are disrupting a child's education.

Most teachers and schools as a whole will try to resolve such matters before calling on the expertise of the EWO, and this service will in fact ask for evidence that this has been done before they get involved with a particular case. The non-attendance at school by a pupil can be the result of a wide range of factors and, as such, other professionals may need to become involved, e.g. social workers.

If a child in your class has a high degree of absence you may find that the school is already aware of the cause, e.g. regular medical appointments, but if the absence is for an unknown reason you would need to discuss your concerns with a senior member of staff. If a pupil in your care makes a disclosure to you on the cause of their absences, it is your duty to report this exactly as the child has relayed it to you.

Other duties carried out by the EWO which may give rise with your liaison with them are:

- regulating child employment;
- advising on child-protection issues;
- helping to arrange alternative educational provision for excluded pupils;
- preparing reports on SEN pupils as part of the statementing process.

Local authority support services

Local authorities offer a range of services to support children with special educational needs and their families, and this starts with schemes specifically designed to support pre-school children.

These include the following.

- Parent partnership services – offering information to help parents make decisions about their child's education, especially during assessment processes.
- Home visiting services – including Early Years inclusion teams, Home Start and Portage (a home visiting educational service which equips parents with the skills to help their child, these visitors can include teachers, OT, nurses and social workers).
- Parent support groups – including those in the voluntary sector.
- Resources and publications – offering advice and links to other organisations.

School-age pupils usually receive support from the local authority professionals listed separately, e.g. EWO, educational psychologist.

National Health Service

School nurses are highly skilled professionals, and are in fact the only trained nurses working between health and education. They provide an essential link between school, home and the community that helps safeguard the well-being of children and young people.

(Teachernet, 2009)

The role of the school nurse has changed greatly over recent times, and the outdated image of the 'nit nurse' has now been replaced by a health professional with impressively wide-ranging responsibilities.

Some of the roles undertaken by a school nurse are as follows.

- Assessing the needs of children when entering formal education at age 5.
- Supporting pupils with complex health needs.
- Running clinics and parenting programmes.
- Running immunisation and vaccination programmes.
- Providing health schemes for children and young people.

School nurses also play a valuable role in the Healthy Schools scheme, which can offer the following.

- Advice to young people to help them manage their own health needs.
- A point of reference for community-based initiatives.
- Support for linking schools to primary care trusts.
- Additional support and resources for schools to support school staff.

School nurses may be based in a clinic but spend a great deal of their time in the community, both in schools and in the homes of children and young people.

Special schools normally have nurses based within the school, and their role includes supervision of medication, specific health needs, e.g. stoma care, and the care of pupils with severe ongoing health needs, e.g. epilepsy. They also assist doctors carrying out medical reviews, and contribute to the annual reviews of pupils with statements of special educational needs.

NSPCC

From the ages of 5 to 16, school is where children spend most of their time – a total of more than 11,000 hours on average.
The NSPCC will be working closely with teachers, parents and local authorities to help develop listening schools where children have someone they can turn to for advice and help.

(Mary Marsh, Chief Executive of the NSPCC, 2000–08).

Historically, this organisation was primarily concerned with the focus of its title, the prevention of cruelty to children. However, this is certainly not the case today, and the NSPCC offers a wide and diverse range of services to support children and young people, which of course still includes the vital support they give to children at risk.

The main focus of the NSPCC in schools is, as the quote states, to provide children and young people with the opportunity to have their voice heard and to address any problems a child may encounter.

The NSPCC undertakes this in the following ways.

- On-site counselling – within local schools.
- Lunchtime walk-in facilities – once again within schools, offering counselling and an information point.
- Peer support/mentoring schemes – help and support with the setting up of these support network schemes which can then be run effectively by the pupils within schools.
- Office-based counselling, advice and advocacy – offering neutral space for children, young people and their family and friends to explore problems.
- Solution talk – self and assisted referral for counselling.
- Counselling service – within schools that do not have dedicated counselling services on site.

The NSPCC also offers valuable resources on anti-bullying, personal safety and peer mediation.

Occupational therapists

The role of the occupational therapist is to assess and treat physical and psychiatric conditions using specific and purposeful activities to prevent or alleviate disability and promote independent functioning. Occupational therapists are often based in hospitals or attached to special schools, and may work with pupils within schools or as an outpatient.

They are often involved in the assessment for, and provision of, wheelchairs or specialist classroom chairs to aid and assist a child's independent mobility issues. They will also give advice and support on difficulties associated with fine motor skills, handwriting and perceptual skills, as well as offering guidance on dressing and feeding.

Pupils who require the input of an occupational therapist may already receive additional support in school, but the advice that occupational therapists can offer to you as a teacher will better equip you when devising effective strategies to a pupil requiring specific occupational support.

Physiotherapists

As with occupational therapists, physiotherapists are based in hospitals or attached to special schools. Their role is to assess and treat physical problems, and their role with a pupil could be short and very specific, e.g. after major surgery or a road accident.

However, their input is usually more long term, involving the treatment of pupils with physical disabilities. As more and more pupils with physical difficulties are being effectively integrated into mainstream education, you can expect to have more contact with a physiotherapist, who as well as providing specialist advice and input, e.g. walking frames, specialist footwear, mobility exercises and hydrotherapy, will also be able to offer support and advice to class staff, in order that the pupil can access a full as possible curriculum.

Pupils who have additional support in class may be able to integrate exercise programmes, etc., into their curriculum (e.g. PE), so enhancing inclusion.

Police and youth offending teams

It can be confidently argued that teachers only hope to liaise with the police and organisations such as the youth offending team in the capacity of classroom support, e.g. road safety or 'stranger danger'. However, it may be the case that pupils in your care or their family members have other associations, and you may need to liaise with the police or supporting organisations in order to meet the needs of the child or young person.

There has been much publicity recently about police actually being based within secondary schools to help improve behaviour and cut truancy. However, Sir Alan Steer who is carrying out an ongoing review of behaviour in schools stated:

> Schools working in partnership with the police service can deal better with community problems and better educate their pupils as responsible members of society.
>
> (Daily Telegraph, 2009)

With this in mind, it becomes clear that effective multidisciplinary working with the police can play a vital role in the overall safeguarding of children and young people, and that the support they can offer can only enhance work already being carried out by teachers.

Services for the hearing impaired

Many pupils have mild to moderate hearing loss often caused by childhood illness, and for the duration of this loss they often cope relatively well, with neither themselves, their parents or others involved in their care actually being aware that a loss exists. However, for some pupils this loss can have a significant effect on their everyday life, especially their ability to cope within a classroom environment. In some circumstances a child with hearing loss copes well at home and it is only when they start school that the problem manifests itself, with the teacher often being the person who identifies the problem.

The majority of local authorities have a service to support pupils with hearing loss, with specialist teachers who are available to visit children and young people in school or at home and offer the support and resources required.

Pupils with a severe loss, or who are profoundly deaf, can access mainstream education with this effective support, while some pupils need the specialist intervention found in a specialist unit or special school.

CASE STUDY
Difficulty hearing instructions
Peter had attended nursery and pre-school provision, and although he did not interact and communicate a great deal with his peers he always seemed happy and his behaviour was good. When he started in a Reception/Year 1 class his behaviour started to deteriorate and the teacher found it very difficult to keep him on task. The work he did produce was not greatly below the expected standards, but was often quite muddled, except for when he copied from his peers, which was becoming a

regular occurrence. From observation by the teacher it became clear that Peter was not hearing, or not hearing clearly and correctly, what both the teacher and his peers were saying. He did not fully understand this situation himself, and as a result began to misbehave in order to detract from the fact that he was unable to complete his work as he could not hear the instructions.

A visit from the teacher for the hearing impaired, and a subsequent hospital visit, very soon rectified the situation, and as well as Peter's behaviour improving the standard of his work did also.

Prior to formal schooling Peter had always managed to cope by picking up on other clues, e.g. body language, facial expression, actions of others, and it was only when he was expected to follow verbal instructions that the problems manifested themselves.

Services for the visually impaired

As with the hearing impaired, most local authorities have a specialist service to support pupils who are visually impaired, again led by specialist teachers. As is so often the case, pupils with a mild sight defect cope quite well before starting school and it is only when the child starts formal education that the problem is identified. Most problems encountered by these pupils can be addressed by the class teacher and specialist teacher, working in conjunction with the parents, to devise and implement strategies and resources to enable the child to learn effectively alongside their peers.

Pupils with severe visual impairments, usually those who are registered as partially sighted or as blind, can still have some vision no matter how limited, and with the appropriate support can access the curriculum. Some pupils, however, do need to attend a special school or a specialist school for the blind in order to have their needs fully met.

It is only after discussion and liaison with this service that decisions as to appropriate placements can be made.

Social workers

The role of the social worker is to work with people who have been socially excluded or who are experiencing crisis. They aim to provide support in order that service users can help themselves. Over 50 per cent of all social workers work with young people and their families.

A great deal of media coverage is often given to high-profile cases, e.g. 'Baby Peter' case, and the role that social workers played within it. However, on a daily basis, social workers are dealing with many cases involving many families and young people, which have very successful and positive outcomes. It can also still often be the case that the involvement of a social worker within a family carries a stigma, and some parents often refuse valuable support and advice because of this.

It will often be the case that for some pupils in your class, there will already be intervention from social workers, either for the pupil or for another family member or the family as a whole. This intervention can take many forms depending on the problems being experienced, and for many families their social worker becomes a trusted friend, who many children will refer to by their first name as they would a family member. It may be the case therefore, that a family or particularly a child who is causing you some concern may already be receiving help from 'Sue' or 'John' that they so readily talk about, and problems are in fact being addressed. The school SENCO/INCO should be able to inform you that this is the case, as multidisciplinary liaison should already be taking place.

Speech and language therapists

The role of the speech and language therapist (SALT) is to promote effective communication for all children and young people. This can encompass a wide and varied range of difficulties, from a child with a slight language delay, to a child with autism who has no speech or method of effective communication. They usually provide services from their base in a health setting, e.g. local health centre, children's clinic, and work in schools and other educational settings. They also can be attached to special school or units which require specialist input, e.g. school for ASD pupils.

As well as their input into effective communication they also work with pupils who have eating or swallowing problems, usually associated with a medical problem.

As a teacher with a pupil experiencing speech and language difficulties, effective liaison with a SALT team member is essential, as the support they can offer and the strategies that they can devise can become an essential tool within the classroom.

Sure Start

This is an integrated Early Years service in which the DCSF encourages the delivery of childcare alongside education, health and family services. It is the aim of this service to provide high-quality, integrated Early Years provision to the heart of communities, and by 2010 there will be 3500 children's centres.

While this provision centres on early childhood, it is also the aim of the service to provide childcare for all children who require it. This provision is for children aged between 3 and 14, between 8am and 6pm each weekday, and by 2010 there will be over 2 million sustainable childcare places for children up to 16, many within the context of extended schools.

As a teacher therefore, you may find that this service becomes 'wrap around care' in conjunction with your own input, and may also extend and enhance work that is being carried out within the classroom.

PRACTICAL TASK PRACTICAL TASK **PRACTICAL TASK** PRACTICAL TASK **PRACTICAL TASK**

Investigate the type of care provision that pupils on your placements receive out of school. Does this enhance or extend the learning that takes place within school?

Organisations which give information and advice

Although you may never have to work in partnership with any of the following, it is useful to know of their existence and how to contact them, in order that you can best support both the children in your care and their families.

- Advisory Centre for Education – independent advice for parents, teachers and governors on all educational matters. **www.ace-ed.org.uk**

- Education Otherwise – support and information to families whose children are educated out of school. **www.education-otherwise.org**
- National Association of Gifted Children – support to parents on how to deal with a gifted child from 18 months to 14 years. **www.nagcbritain.org.uk**
- Young Minds – a service for parents of children or young people experiencing difficulties at school owing to mental health problems. **www.youngminds.org.uk**
- Parentline Plus – providing support to anyone looking after a child, with a free confidential helpline. **www.parentlineplus.org.uk**
- Centre for Studies on Inclusive Education – information and advice for SEN pupils up to age 19. **www.csie.org.uk**
- The Council for Disabled Children – information service to parents and professionals on the needs of disabled children and young people. **www.ncb.org.uk/cdc**
- Parents for Inclusion - information, advice and support to parents of children with learning difficulties. **www.parentsforinclusion.org**
- RNID – information to the deaf and hard of hearing. **www.mid.org.uk**
- RNIB – information to the blind and visually impaired. **www.rnib.org.uk**

A SUMMARY OF **KEY POINTS**

> This chapter has given you a brief overview of some of the outside agencies and the role they can play in supporting a child that you teach. Some individuals are now arguing that in some cases there are too many different individuals involved in a child's care, and that parents would possibly prefer only one point of contact for all matters relating to their child. It will be interesting to see if this becomes the case within the structure we have in place at the present time.

> It is clear, however, that in some cases, many professionals will need to be involved in the lives of the pupils you teach, and that you need to become familiar with working in a multidisciplinary team. In many cases it will be the schools SENCO/INCO who will instigate and carry out this process, although it still remains your responsibility to meet the needs of the pupils in your care by whatever means.

MOVING *ON* > > > > > > MOVING *ON* > > > > > > MOVING *ON*

Always view the intervention of outside agencies and multidisciplinary working as a positive part of your teaching career. Nobody is yet claiming that we have 'got it right', but if you become adept at this way of working, the process becomes nearer to meeting its objectives, which is to ensure that the five outcomes of Every Child Matters are successful for every child.

REFERENCES REFERENCES **REFERENCES** REFERENCES **REFERENCES** REFERENCES

Barnados (2009) **www.barnardos.org.uk/whatwedo/ourprojects** (accessed 30.10.09).

DfES (2001) *Special Educational Needs – Code of Practice*. Nottingham: DfES.

DfES (2004) *ECM: Change for children*. Nottingham: DfES.

Daily Telegraph (2009) **www.telegraph.co.uk/education/educationnews/4538019** (accessed 5.10.09).

TDA (2008) *Special educational needs and/or disabilities, Training toolkit*. London: TDA.

Teachernet (2009) **www.teachernet.gov.uk/teachingandlearning/library/schoolnurses** (accessed 30.10.09).

www.dcsf.gov.uk/everychildmatters/ete/behaviourinschools/supportservices (accessed 30.10.09).

www.dcsf.gov.uk/everychildmatters/healthandwellbeing/mentalhealthissues/camhs (accessed 8.10.09).

www.dcsf.gov.uk/everychildmatters/youth/youthjustice/policeservice (accessed 8.10.09).

www.dcsf.gov.uk/everychildmatters/earlyyears/surestart (accessed 30.10.09).

www.dcsf.gov.uk/publications/childrensplan (accessed 5.10.09).

www.ican.org.uk/talkingpoint/related%20topics/national%20service%20framework (accessed 7.10.09).

www.nspcc.org.uk/whatwedo/servicesforchildreandfamilies (accessed 5.10.09).

www.direct.gov.uk/en/parents/preschooldevelopmentandlearning/specialeducationalneeds (accessed 30.10.09).

www.teachernet.gov.uk/wholeschool/behaviour/attendance (accessed 30.10.09).

FURTHER READING FURTHER READING **FURTHER READING** FURTHER READING

Barker, R. (2009) *Making sense of Every Child Matters: multi professional practice guidance*. Bristol: Policy Press.

Cheminais, R. (2006) *Every Child Matters – a practical guide for teachers*. London: David Fulton.

Cheminais, R. (2007) *How to achieve the Every Child Matters standards: a practical guide*. London: Paul Chapman.

Miller, L. (2009) *Working with children in the early years*. London: Routledge.

Spooner, W. (2006) *The SEN handbook for trainee teachers, NQTs and TAs*. London: David Fulton.

Todd, L. (2007) *Partnerships for inclusive education: a critical approach to collaborative working*. London: Routledge Falmer.

Useful websites

www.camh.org.uk
www.library.nhs.uk/mentalhealth
www.nspcc.org.uk
www.barnardos.org.uk
www.everychildmatters.gov.uk
www.teachernet.gov.uk
www.direct.gov.uk

10
Creating learner-friendly environments

Chapter objectives

By the end of this chapter you should be able to:

- **understand how the term 'inclusion' applies to the work of a school;**
- **know about the Salamanca Statement (UNESCO,1994);**
- **know about the importance of modifying planning and teaching styles and the necessity to build access strategies into your teaching;**
- **understand the importance of collaboration and co-operative working;**
- **know how to identify barriers and make learning challenges faced by pupils feasible;**
- **make reasonable adjustments for a range of learning barriers.**

This chapter addresses the following Professional Standards for the award of QTS:

Q1, Q2, Q3a, Q21a

Introduction

This chapter provides guidance on how to create learner-friendly environments to support all learners. The chapter addresses the need to consider the adaptation of teaching styles, developing access strategies to overcome barriers to learning as well as the modification of learning objectives to meet individual needs.

How the term inclusion applies to the work of a school

Creating an atmosphere that motivates children to learn is always a priority. Classroom teachers and assistants within the classroom are responsible for creating a learning environment where all pupils can be included in the learning process in a supportive and purposeful way.

Creating learner-friendly environments within our school system will help learners to feel safe, happy and welcome, thus enabling them to make good progress. Essentially learner-friendly environments allow all children to enjoy a quality education where all aspects of the curriculum are accessible, yet pupil individuality is both welcomed and appreciated. If you want to get the best out of your learners this must be a major focus of your work.

Legislation states that no child should be excluded from participating or learning in the classroom environment and that every attempt must be made to help individuals who may be developing or have developed learning barriers. The Disability Discrimination Act places a statutory duty for schools to make reasonable adjustments to cater for the needs of disabled learners and the Statutory Framework for Inclusion in the National Curriculum emphasises the need to identify and remove barriers to learning and participation. This process ensures equality of opportunity. All teachers must therefore ensure that any barriers to pupils' learning are identified and eradicated. This might involve some or all of the following processes.

- Carefully differentiating the task in a range of ways.
- Building in access strategies.
- Using a range of teaching strategies.

These elements will be examined in more detail in this chapter.

Developing an inclusive classroom

It is essential that you provide a welcoming environment for all learners. However, it is difficult to pinpoint the precise characteristics of an inclusive teacher because a commitment to inclusive practice demands a value-led, principled approach. 'Values' is very much part of the inclusion debate and inclusive teachers do not disassociate their practice from their values and principles. It is therefore suggested that you spend some time reflecting on your own values and principles in terms of inclusion. You surely cannot pretend to believe in inclusion. If you do this you will not have a genuine commitment to it. You have to believe that all children are important and deserve the best education, even those with challenging behaviour. This commitment to all learners must be deeply embedded within you so that your practice is true to your values and principles.

In order to develop an inclusive classroom you have a responsibility to model inclusive values. You need to demonstrate that you respect all children and adults in the setting. You need to provide a welcoming environment where parents feel welcome and are encouraged to come into the setting. Parents should be provided with opportunities to express their own views and they should be empowered to influence policies within the setting. The classroom environment should show images that reflect difference and diversity, for example through images depicting different races and cultures. Classroom resources should also reflect difference and diversity.

I was saddened to hear of a secondary school teacher stating publicly that children with behavioural difficulties did not deserve to be educated in mainstream settings because of the impact of their behaviour on other learners. This teacher had never considered that the behavioural issues might be a response to particular pedagogical approaches that these learners had been subjected to. Resistance can be challenging, yet invigorating. It can energise us to rethink our own practice. Inclusive teachers continuously reflect on their practice and refine it in order to achieve the best outcomes for all learners.

All children need to feel as though they belong. This is a key element of inclusive practice. In addition, teachers should celebrate pupils' diversity. Diversity is something which should be neither hidden nor ridiculed. It is a positive feature of life and life would be very dull if we were all the same. Children have a right to be taught in a supportive environment where they are able to make mistakes without fear of ridicule from either peers or adults. An inclusive ethos will prevail in classrooms where there is evidence of much co-operative learning. Children should be encouraged to be mutually supportive of children with special educational needs and understand that that they can all play a part in helping one another. A classroom environment which encourages competition is not inclusive. This will serve only to create winners and losers and the losers are often those with special educational needs (Cole, 2005).

Your learners will develop in different directions. Some learners thrive in academic areas, while some excel at sports or others have strengths within creative and performing arts. As an inclusive teacher it is your role to find the strengths within each child and to celebrate these. This will undoubtedly have a positive impact on pupils' self-esteem. In an inclusive classroom, teachers, other adults and learners are partners in the learning process. There are no hierarchies. Inclusive teachers aim to develop learners' confidence and focus on making pupils feel good about their efforts. All progress is recognised and celebrated, no matter how small it may appear.

Inclusive classrooms are warm, friendly and full of fun and laughter. This is the essence of quality learning. Children surely do not learn if they are intimidated, stressed or made to feel that they are worthless. Think of your learners as a root system. In inclusive classrooms the 'roots' are allowed to grow in many different directions but there are no hierarchies. The roots are joined together in a mutually supportive way (adapted from Goodley, 2007). In this way all learners can thrive and everyone grows and develops.

Inclusive schools

Unfortunately the standards agenda seems to value academic learning in narrowly defined parameters over other types of learning. This creates a system which effectively fails those learners who can never achieve high standards within the academic domain. In the current system some learners are allowed to flourish and the growth of other learners is stilted. Some win and some lose and the education system places unrealistic pressure on those learners with special educational needs to achieve the same norms as others (see for example the work of Lloyd, 2008, and Armstrong, 2005). The system marginalises learners with special educational needs by focusing heavily on reaching national norms in narrow areas such as literacy and numeracy. There is nothing wrong with high standards and we must not have low expectations of any learner. However, the standards that we set our learners do need to be realistic and achievable and we should celebrate the smallest signs of progress, even if the steps are very tiny to us. To a child, these steps might be enormous.

We should also celebrate achievement across the full breadth of the curriculum. A child with Asperger syndrome may learn slowly to play co-operatively with his/her peers. In terms of progress, this is outstanding. However, in terms of attainment this child may be labelled as a failure if he/she is unable to achieve national standards in specific areas of the curriculum. Inclusive schools challenge this system and value all steps in learning in different aspects of the curriculum.

Inclusive schools do not seek to normalise learners. Children with ASD may not want to play co-operatively with their peers or be forced to carry out group tasks. They may prefer to work or play alone. These learners should not be forced to conform. Systems within schools and classrooms therefore need to be sufficiently flexible to cater for the needs of all learners. Some children with ASD may not be able to sit through a ten-minute carpet session. They may need something to manipulate in their hands while they take part in whole-class sessions to enable them to concentrate without being disruptive, for example, a piece of modelling dough. Some learners may need extra support within lessons or additional resources to help them access the learning. You might need to develop different boundaries of acceptable behaviour for individual learners. It is clear that one uniform set of rules for a whole class, or indeed school, may not be the best way of developing an inclusive ethos.

Learner-friendly environments develop highly positive and secure relationships with all learners. The focus should be consistently on developing in learners a positive sense of self and good self-image. To develop effective partnerships with learners you need to find ways of consulting in order to give them a voice. *Every Child Matters* stresses the importance of pupil participation in decision-making processes. Find out what their interests are and take account of these during the planning process. If children feel upset or rejected then they will not feel included. Teachers have a statutory duty to keep children safe and all forms of bullying should be challenged.

UNESCO's Salamanca Statement (1994)

The 1994 world conference of the United Nations Educational, Scientific and Cultural Organisation (UNESCO) agreed that inclusion should be the norm. A new framework for action was adopted, advising that ordinary schools should accommodate *all children, regardless of their physical, intellectual, social, emotional, linguistic or other conditions*. It was highlighted that by creating learner-friendly environments, disabled children could attend the neighbourhood school *that would be attended if the child did not have a disability'* (UNESCO, 1994).

Identifying barriers and making learning challenges feasible

The Disability Discrimination Act states that no child should be excluded from participating or learning in the classroom environment and that every attempt must be made to help individuals who may be developing or have developed learning barriers. This should be done by making reasonable adjustments to classroom provision.

REFLECTIVE TASK

Consider the following examples and how a pupil may be excluded from participation if unable to:

- see the interactive whiteboard;
- hear the teacher;
- read a text or book;
- access the computer;
- contribute in a talk session.
- Add further examples to the list given above and further consider how these barriers may be reduced.
- Consider how these barriers could be grouped. Using physical, social/emotional, intellectual and communication domains, start to identify the issues.

Developing learner-friendly environments

Ofsted have identified specific criteria to enable schools to evaluate their practice in relation to inclusion. According to Ofsted (2004), in inclusive schools:

- pupils make good progress in relation to their starting points and their achievements are in line with those of pupils with similar difficulties;

- the curriculum enables all pupils to learn and prepares them for the next stage of education and for the opportunities and responsibilities of adult life;
- the teaching enables the pupils to learn and inspires them to think for themselves and enjoy learning;
- the pupils make a positive contribution to the school community;
- the school reviews its policy and practice on inclusion.

Inclusion in practice can be addressed through:

- choosing appropriate learning objectives;
- modifying teaching styles;
- building in access strategies to remove potential barriers to learning.

Choosing appropriate learning objectives

When planning for learners with special educational needs your starting point must be what your learners already know and can do. This knowledge will come from accurate assessment information, much of which will be formative. There is sufficient flexibility within the National Curriculum for teachers to select objectives from earlier or later key stages and some children may still need to work on developmental milestones within the Early Years Foundation Stage framework.

Sometimes it will be inappropriate for learners with SEN to work on the same learning objectives as their peers. In these circumstances you should take the decision that these learners need to focus on different learning objectives which more sharply address their needs.

However, in some cases it is possible that learners with SEN may be able to work on the same learning objectives as their peers if appropriate access strategies are built into the task to enable them to access the learning. In some circumstances learners with SEN might be able to achieve these learning objectives if adaptations are made to the teaching style. In other situations learners with SEN may be quite capable of working on the same theme as their peers but following objectives which are earlier in a sequence of progression.

PRACTICAL TASK PRACTICAL TASK **PRACTICAL TASK** PRACTICAL TASK **PRACTICAL TASK**

Identify a learning objective from the Primary Mathematics Framework for children in Year 2. Now identify an earlier objective in the framework which comes before this objective. Share your ideas with a colleague. Now repeat this task for literacy.

You need to be flexible in your approach and take decisions about which learning objectives are suitable and which are inappropriate. However, in all situations you should maintain consistently high expectations of all learners in your class. Most learners with special educational needs will have an Individual Education Plan which identifies clear learning goals. Ideally these should have been negotiated with the parents or carers and the child. You should aim to take these learning goals into account when you plan for learners with additional needs. Some targets on the IEP may need to be addressed individually with the child but some can be met through whole-class sessions, depending on the specific target. Some children will have very specific targets on IEPs which cannot be met through whole-class sessions or group work. In these circumstances it may be necessary to withdraw the child from the classroom from time to time to allow them to work on their targets with adult supervision.

Learners with SEN may work on:

- the same objectives as the rest of the class, providing adaptations are made;
- linked learning objectives which follow the same theme which the rest of the class are following but that has been appropriately differentiated to meet the needs of learners with SEN;
- distinct and different learning where pupils work on their individual targets alongside others in the classroom;
- alternative work (usually out of class).

(TDA, 2008)

Modifying teaching styles and approaches

Some learners with SEN will need different resources to enable them to access the learning, thus removing barriers to participation and achievement. The nature of the adaptation will clearly depend on the individual needs of each child. As a rule of thumb you should aim to make the teaching experience as multi-sensory as possible. Provide learners with as many opportunities to use their senses. Children with ASD may respond to visual approaches in your teaching. Learners with reading difficulties may respond to kinaesthetic approaches when learning the sounds that letters make. The main point is that if you embed visual, auditory and kinaesthetic approaches into your teaching, this is likely to result in more meaningful learning as opposed to traditional didactic approaches.

CASE STUDY
A multi-sensory approach
Jabina struggles to differentiate between initial phonemes. After discussion with her parents it was decided to send home a phonics CD based on repetition of sounds and kinaesthetic actions to accompany the sounds. This enabled Jabina to be supported by her parents who were also developing an understanding of the English alphabetic code. This was further reinforced with simple dice games in the classroom and a multi-sensory tactile approach.

REFLECTIVE TASK

Can you think of other resources that could be loaned or put into a story sack/game sack to further support Jabina?

PRACTICAL TASK PRACTICAL TASK PRACTICAL TASK PRACTICAL TASK PRACTICAL TASK

In literacy you are focusing on the structure and features of recounts with a class of Year 2 children. You have a child with learning and cognition difficulties and he is unable to write. Discuss with a colleague how you might adapt your teaching style for this child to enable him to access the key learning.

Simple adaptations such as the use of a number line in mathematics or a word mat in literacy can help children to access learning.

Developing access strategies

Simple access strategies can enable learners with SEN to access the learning that the rest of the class is doing. Some suggestions that you might try are listed below.

- Pre-teach pupils before the lesson so that they can make good progress in the lesson.
- Make good use of ICT, for example a child may be unable to write but may be able to use a word processor to put down their ideas; they might be able to record their ideas on a Dictaphone or you might be able to purchase specialist software which can convert speech to text.
- Allow learners to work with a classroom assistant or teacher.
- Allow learners to work with a study buddy.
- Find alternative ways of recording. If writing is a barrier to learning, the pupils might be able to present evidence of their learning through making a video, taking photographs of their learning or using images.
- Ensure that pupils have access to resources that will support them in their learning, e.g. spellings, number squares, number lines and dictionaries.

This is not an exhaustive list and you will be able to add to it to cater for the specific needs of the learners in your class. The National Curriculum inclusion statement states that schools have a statutory duty to set suitable learning challenges, respond to pupils' diverse learning needs and overcome potential barriers to learning and assessment. The strategies suggested above will help you to achieve these points. Some barriers to learning can be attitudinal. Staff and other pupils may have negative attitudes towards learners with SEN. This will certainly not contribute to an inclusive ethos. Some barriers may be physical, such as a child needing a specially designed chair or special pair of scissors to enable them to complete a task. Some barriers may be organisational and it is the responsibility of the school to ensure that SEN provision (staffing) is appropriately deployed throughout the school to enable learners with SEN equality of opportunity.

CASE STUDY

Adaptive technologies

Sadie has limited language skills and cannot communicate using words. Other children experience difficulties communicating with her and are unwilling to play with her. The school has contacted the speech and language therapist who now comes into the school on a regular basis. One of the devices recommended was a USB keyboard overlay. The teaching assistant was asked to attend a training course so that she could learn how to use the equipment. The equipment was programmed using overlays of pictures linked to sounds that when pressed omitted simple speech. Sadie was able to use the equipment to communicate further and showed that she was able to make simple choices. In addition the equipment generated interest from the other pupils in the class who also wanted to work with the equipment.

REFLECTIVE TASK

Think of ways in which technological modifications could be used to aid other pupils with additional needs.

When you are next on placement, discuss with the ICT co-ordinator or the ICT technician the range of adaptive technologies available to support learners with special educational needs.

Have a commitment to collaboration and co-operative school working. Creating such an inclusive environment is not always easy and requires careful detailed planning. There is no 'one fix' or 'quick fix' methodology to follow. However, the responsibility does not lie with the classroom teacher alone and a working group could form to gather useful information and ideas to consider possible changes and developments.

Explore the people who could be considered in such a group. A map of ideas or list of names can be made.

In your placement school speak to the SENCO about the range of people who support learners with special educational needs and try to find opportunities to shadow one of these professionals.

The size and geographical orientation of such a group will depend on the purpose and to some extent the reason for the adjustments to be made within the learning environment. Clearly this could be on a local scale such as a single classroom to meet the needs of a specific group or individual pupils, or on a wider national or international scale, depending on the adjustments made and the impact on a wider audience.

A good place to start on a local level would be to consider an ideal or 'dream' environment and then to make what provision is possible or 'reasonable' within a given situation. Thus by identifying the needs and creating a 'vision' it will be possible to produce a plan of action.

REFLECTIVE TASK

Consider which aspects would contribute to your dream learner-friendly environment for a target group of pupils or an individual pupil with specific needs.

Do all schools have inclusive learner-friendly environments?

People assume that schools are purpose-built for the number, age and type of pupils they educate. However, in practice you will find that this is not the case and environments have to be adapted to make them as learner-friendly as possible.

Inclusive environments should include the elements of good classroom practice. For example, they should be:

- comfortable;
- welcoming;
- well lit;

- friendly not stifling;
- spacious;
- calm;
- well organised.

Developing an inclusive, learning-friendly environment

An inclusive learning-friendly environment should benefit the whole school community.

Children

In inclusive environments children gain confidence and have high self-esteem. They are able to work independently and develop creativity, which benefits the learning across the curriculum. They feel able to ask for help and their attempts to produce work and answer questions are valued and not ridiculed. In inclusive schools pupils' self-respect grows as children gain confidence to work independently and they learn to communicate better with others both inside and outside the school. Learners develop respect for others, and value achievements made.

Teachers

With collaboration, teachers expand their knowledge and understanding of how to meet the needs of learners with special educational needs. These inclusive teachers seek further professional training to update their knowledge and skills and they value a multidisciplinary approach. They challenge stereotypical responses and become more creative as they search for ways of addressing pupils' individual learning needs. Inclusive teachers seek feedback from parents and carers as well as pupils and colleagues. They are prepared to modify their practices to cater for pupils' individuality. Effective teachers can empathise with pupils and they are able to develop new ideas and techniques. In addition they are willing to try new technologies to address pupils' needs. Inclusive teachers make very effective use of classroom support, helpers and outside agencies as they develop their inclusive practice. They value the very small steps that some children take and they celebrate these so that the children begin to feel important and develop a feeling of self-worth.

Parents

Many parents of pupils with SEN start to take an active role in their children's education. These parents welcome the fact that their children are valued and made welcome in a supportive learning environment. Many become involved and contribute willingly to reviews of progress. However, some parents may be reluctant to develop home–school partnerships and schools will need to find ways of reaching these parents. Above all, a sense of pride in their child's progress must develop.

Parents have told us that good, honest and open communication is one of the important components of building confidence and good relationships. Face-to-face communication with parents, treating them as equal partners with expertise in their children's needs is crucial to establishing and sustaining confidence. Where things go wrong, the root causes can often be traced to poor communication between school, local authority and parent.

(Lamb Inquiry, 2009)

The community

By fostering a community approach, better relationships develop and the pride felt by many children, parents and teachers spreads into the wider community. People from wider social backgrounds are willing to participate and become involved in the activities of a school. They may also work with individual pupils.

CASE STUDY

Access strategies

Michael was made redundant. He had previously worked as a joiner. The teacher approached Michael to see if he would be interested in working with small groups and individuals, supporting them to use tools for design and technology. Initially Michael was reluctant but after meeting with other helpers in the school he realised that he had a lot to offer. He was able to go into school one afternoon a week and support small groups of children making buggies. Michael was able to introduce the children to new skills and the teacher valued his knowledge and support. Michael further considered the difficulty of holding and cutting wood and was able to make simple modifications to the task to enable a learner with motor neurone problems to access the activity. He devised a cutting sleeve to hold the saw so that the child was able to control it.

REFLECTIVE TASK

- What are the advantages of developing community links to support learners with special educational needs?
- Think of adjustments that you could make to enable such a learner to access practical activities, such as sewing, cooking and painting.

Barriers to inclusion

This section briefly examines the barriers to inclusion and the facilitators of effective inclusion.

PRACTICAL TASK PRACTICAL TASK PRACTICAL TASK PRACTICAL TASK PRACTICAL TASK

Read the following quotes from teachers and discuss the key barriers and facilitators to effective inclusion.

We've got a teacher who sees his job as just to teach. He expects every child to conform and that is against inclusion. You can't have a child coming in with behaviour problems and the teacher not recognising

these problems. It is the difference between – if there is a problem in the classroom . . . blaming the child, or thinking . . . what can I do to make this easier? Or what is wrong with my environment if I am not meeting this child's needs. That is a massive difference. Teaching styles have a lot to do with it. Inclusion is harder if you just want them all to sit there quietly. (Teacher 1)

Some one-to-one sessions are appropriate. It's the idea of one-to-one in terms of one child; one adult and they stick together all day, every day. We see it happening in our school. This is hopeless because if a child has someone next to them all the time you are setting them apart from all of the others. The child will become dependent. (Teacher 2)

Some teachers don't plan for children with SEN or assess them. They don't know what they need to know next. They leave it all up to the support staff and these children are educated solely by teaching assistants outside classrooms. (Teacher 3)

You can raise standards if you ignore the rest and work with your middle groups. These are the children who some teachers target. I don't, I give them all time, but some teachers just teach the middle ones and hold the others. You hear them talking about it in the staff room. (Teacher 4)

When we had Freya we had to fight to get a guard to support her with swimming. She had cerebral palsy. Eventually we got one and he lowered her into the pool. She loved it. However, it took months and months to get to that stage. (Teacher 5)

Some children get tarred with a brush by the way other parents and some children react to them. One parent has withdrawn her child as a result of a boy in my class. She saw me three times, before her child joined the school, to discuss the child she was concerned about. She didn't give him a chance. She blamed everything on him and always pointed the finger at him. Eventually she took her child out of school because she said this child was always bullying her child. In actual fact it was both of them. At least now the child has a chance. The child who has gone knew how to press his buttons. (Teacher 6)

(Glazzard, 2006)

REFLECTIVE TASK

- What are your views on segregated one-to-one support?
- Do you think the inclusion agenda can work within the context of broader educational policy and the overarching standards agenda?
- How can teacher attitude impact on the creation of inclusive environments?

A SUMMARY OF **KEY POINTS**

> **Learning objectives may need to be modified to meet the needs of all learners.**

> **Learning can be accessible to all children with the implementation of carefully considered and appropriate access strategies.**

> **The careful consideration of multi-sensory approaches can effectively address the needs of all learners.**

> **Positive attitudes by staff towards inclusive education are conducive to positive outcomes for all learners.**

MOVING *ON* > > > > > > **MOVING** *ON* > > > > > > **MOVING** *ON*

In your placement school take the opportunity to reflect upon access strategies used by teachers across the curriculum. Consider the following questions in relation to one pupil.
- What are the barriers to learning?
- Do these access strategies meet the needs of the child?
- Consider additional strategies to support and enhance the learning of this child.

REFERENCES REFERENCES **REFERENCES** REFERENCES **REFERENCES** REFERENCES

Armstrong, D. (2005) 'Reinventing "inclusion": New Labour and the cultural politics of special education', *Oxford Review of Education,* 31 (1), 135–151.

Cole, B. (2005) 'Good faith and effort? Perspectives on educational inclusion', *Disability and Society,* 20 (3), 331–344.

Glazzard, J. (2006) *Rhetoric or Reality? The Facilitators and Barriers to Inclusion in one Primary School.* Unpublished MEd dissertation, University of Manchester.

Goodley, D. (2007) 'Towards socially just pegagogies: Deluzoguattarian critical disability studies', *International Journal of Inclusive Education,* 11 (3), 317–334.

Lamb, B. (2009) *Lamb Inquiry: Special Educational Needs and Parental Confidence.* Nottingham: DCSF Publications.

Lloyd, C. (2008) 'Removing barriers to achievement: A strategy for inclusion or exclusion?', *International Journal of Inclusive Education,* 12 (2), 221–236.

Ofsted (2004) *Special Educational Needs and Disability: Towards Inclusive Schools.* Manchester: OFSTED Publications.

TDA (2008), *Special educational needs and/or disabilities: A training resource for initial teacher training providers: primary undergraduate courses.* London: TDA.

United Nations Educational, Scientific and Cultural Organisation (UNESCO) (1994) *World Conference on Special Needs Education: Access and Quality.* Paris: UNESCO.

FURTHER READING FURTHER READING **FURTHER READING** FURTHER READING

Ainscow, M., Booth, T., Dyson, A. (2006) *Improving Schools, Developing Inclusion.* Abingdon: Taylor and Frances.

Armstrong, F. and Moore, M. (2004) *Action Research for Inclusive Education: Changing Places, Changing Practices, Changing Minds.* Oxford: RoutledgeFalmer.

Knowles, G. (2006) (ed) *Supporting Inclusive Practice.* London: David Fulton.
    This is an excellent text. It is clear, concise and offers support and advice to practitioners. The book considers practical strategies to support a range of learning needs.

Nutbrown, C. and Clough, P (2005) *Inclusion in the Early Years.* London: SAGE.

Ross-Watt, F. (2005) 'Inclusion and the Early Years: From rhetoric to reality', *Child Care in Practice,* 11 (2), 103–118.

Thomas, G. and Loxley, A. (2007) *Deconstructing Special Education and Constructing Inclusion.* Maidenhead: Open University Press.

Thomas, G. and Vaughan, M. (2004), *Inclusive Education: Readings and Reflections.* Maidenhead: Open University Press.

Topping, K. and Maloney, S. (eds) (2004) *The RoutledgeFalmer Reader in Inclusive Education.* London: RoutledgeFalmer.

Warnock, M. (1978) *Special Educational Needs, Report of the Committee of Enquiry into the Education of Handicapped Children and Young People.* London: HMSO.

Useful websites

www.teachernet.gov.uk/wholeschool/sen/schools/accessibility

Centre for Studies on Inclusive Education **http://inclusion.uwe.ac.uk/csie/csiehome.htm**

Index

Added to the page reference 'f' denotes a figure.